9 FRUITS OF THE SPIRIT

Ralph Sanders

GoToPublish LLC
1-888-337-1724
www.gotopublish.com
info@gotopublish.com

CONTENTS

THE BEGINNING

"The steps of a good man are ordered by the LORD, and He delights in his way."

- Psalms 37:23

Today's Scripture doesn't say God suggested our steps. No, God is strategic. Before you were formed in your mother's womb, He laid out a specific plan for you. Nothing happens randomly. The good breaks and the times you see favor as well as the closed doors and disappointments are a part of God's plan. If you don't understand that, you'll be frustrated when things don't go your way, upset because somebody does you wrong. In reality, these were ordained by God as setups to move you up to a new level of your destiny. Of course we all experienced different types of suffering and pain. We all have felt the pressure of losing are minds trying to hold on to the promises we read about or heard from others. I'm here to share with you on the 9 fruits of the spirit and how they can change your direction & steps in the world we are placed in together! Sin is always in the way and knocking at your door! How can we stop this force of danger coming are way?

You are not at the mercy of fate, or luck, or other people. God has ordered your steps. Do you think a jealous coworker, a bad break, or a closed door can stop or change what God has ordered for you? Those negative circumstances and people are pawns in the hand of God. The enemy thinks he's using them to hold you back; the truth is that God is using them to push you forward. Don't be disappointed when you fall or feel you can't get up or fight the good fight of faith.

Father, thank You that You never allow anything if it's not going to work for my good. Thank You that You purposefully order my steps in the way that is best for me. I believe that what the enemy thinks is holding me back is what You are using to push me forward. It's not always easy to walk in his Devine fruits of Grace he gifted us with to grab hold and walk in them!

Love, joy, peace, goodness and kindness are all supernatural expressions of the character and presence of God fruits who lives inside us. When we yield to them, the Holy Spirit enhances and strengthens them in us to become a river of living water that flows out of us to help bless others!

How can We walk in the Spirit?

Paul writes in **Galatians 5:16**, "I say then: Walk in the Spirit, and you shall not fulfill the lust of the flesh." We all struggle with sin and it is the sting of death. That's a terrible feeling to be caught up into the sinful lifestyle rather than the fruits of Gods labor for are lives here on earth.

The flesh is the expression the Bible uses for the dwelling place of everything in a person that opposes God and His will.

Our ego is like a command center, sending out countless signals and actions. The signals and actions from this command center all revolve around taking care of yourself, preserving your ego, getting honor and favor, and exalting yourself at others' expense.

Human nature would rather sin than suffer, so how do we take up the battle against sin to hold fast to the 9 fruits of the Holy Spirit?

This is something that we have all inherited and are born with, as Adam and Eve's descendants. It is not guilt, but the tendency or inclination to follow our own self-will rather than God's will. We experience this tendency every time we are tempted by our lusts and desires to commit sin. However, *this is where the fight against sin lies!*

You experience temptation when a thought comes to your mind and you are aware that to act according to that impulse would be wrong. You come to a moment of decision: will I choose to sin here, or will I choose to overcome sin? Everyone is tempted when they are drawn away by their own desires and enticed. (**James 1:4**) A temptation is always conscious. You are aware that to give in to this thought would be to sin; to do what you know to be wrong. And it's important to remember that you can't be tempted without the thought first coming into your mind. That is the temptation, not sin you have committed!

It has to do with your attitude: What do you want more? Eternal life with Jesus, or the passing pleasure of sin? That always has to be in your mind, then you will never agree with the thought that is coming into your mind. Go to God in humility and pray, "God, give me strength to stand here and to not give in. I am weak, but You are strong! Give me grace to overcome." You can't overcome without power from Him; You need His grace to be victorious. And then of course He gives you that power. "For the eyes of the Lord run to and fro throughout the whole earth, to show Himself strong on behalf of those whose heart is loyal to Him." **2 Chronicles 2:9** "You can't stop a temptation from coming in to your thoughts, but you can disagree with it and stop it from coming in to and affecting your spirit."

Even when the temptation lasts for a long time. When there is something in you that fights for life, and wants the opposite of God's will. That is your flesh trying to assert itself. It can feel like the temptation is going on and on and on, but it is important to understand that as long as you are fighting it, you are not sinning. If you are consciously saying, "No! I will not do this thing I am tempted to. I will not get angry, I will not be envious, I will not allow impure thoughts," then you are not sinning! No matter how long the temptation lasts.

To engage in battle is to give up every single thing that God points out to you as necessary to give up that would come between yourself and your goal – to be conformed to the image of Christ so that you can be with Him for eternity. Your honor, your will, your desires, your thoughts. All of it must be given up to live according to God's will for your life. It's a desperate longing for the fruits of the spirit to shine in you and control your life rather than your own desires to fall prey to sin nature!

Because the lusts and desires in your flesh are demanding something other than God's will, denying them satisfaction will cause suffering in the flesh, which you will feel acutely. To be faithful requires a firm and decided mindset. You have to acknowledge that nothing good comes from the flesh. (**Romans 7:18**) will explain that nature of course we all fall into! This takes zeal, a determination, and a profound dependency on help from God. You have to be aware of how weak you are as a natural person, how powerless you are against sin, and come to the point where you humbly acknowledge that without God you can do nothing. When you are at that point then you will understand why it is written about Jesus that He prayed until His sweat came like great drops of blood. (**Luke 22:41**)

Jesus was the Son of God, yet He Himself as a man had to pray with vehement cries and tears to God to receive the strength required to sustain Him in battle. That's the spirit you also need to be in. A desperate need for help, a desperate longing to be saved from the sin that you find that so easily ensnares you. (**Hebrews 12:1**) It will also take crying out to God in prayer for you to be saved from sin. You need to pray to get the mind that was in Jesus, the mind to be willing to suffer in the flesh and endure in the battle to put sin to death and walk in his fruits of blessings!

We can usually control our flesh to a degree – at least when the impulses of flesh do not benefit our ego. For the most part, however, our human nature is subject to the powers of the flesh. Therefore when the negative characteristics we inherited through generations present themselves, we often hear, "We are only human."

However, Paul wrote that by walking in the Spirit you no longer need to fulfill these lusts. When you walk in the Spirit you think and act differently than other people in the various situations of life. This does not mean we are better or worse than anyone else at all. We are called to bring all we can to the light of Jesus and his Grace.

VIEW OF THE SPIRIT

"Therefore, put on every piece of God's armor so you will be able to resist the enemy in the time of evil. Then after the battle you will still be standing firm."

- Ephesians 6:13

My interpretation as a believer fighting the good fight of faith is sometimes questionable when feeling weak or walking in the flesh. Sometimes our mind plays games with us and tries to confuse us that we are not in the Spirit of God.

Do you have days where you ask yourself if you have a soul connection with the Holy Spirit and are walking toward the right path? The path He wants you to take. There are days when we struggle to beat our inner demons and recognize the "fruit of the Spirit." And there is no doubt that most Christians have had their struggles, but let's look at things from a different perspective! There are essential dynamics, benefits, and costs to the fruit of the Holy Spirit, as well as results and prices to the works of the flesh that can turn out to be 'false fruits.'

I remember reading about the parable of the sower. The Lord says "the seed" is the Word of God, and "the ground" represents the hearts the seed is sown into.

My understanding is that if I thought only inside the box and not outside it, I would have never understood what God was trying to convey to me; reaching out of the Bible and into my mind to help me realize that the seed is a significant factor for growth.

Jesus gave the interpretation to the Disciples regarding the parable of the seed and the sower:

"Now, the parable is something we should all read and admit its truth. The seed is the word of God! Those by the wayside are the ones who hear; then the Devil comes and takes the word out of their hearts, lest they should believe and be saved. But the ones on the rock are those who, when they hear, receive the word with joy; they have no root, believe for a while, and, in time of temptation, fall away. Now the ones that fell among thorns are those who, when they have heard, go out and are choked with cares, riches, and pleasures of life, and bring no fruit to maturity."

Do you feel this way sometimes? The Bible guides us about wrongdoers and keeping away from distractions. But most of us can relate to this; we fall for worldly temptations. It warns us about being watchful and avoiding things that destroy our souls.

We have to make sure we hear God's voice rather than the voice of the Deceiver who likes to rob, kill, destroy, and damage our faith in the Lord.

> *"Ye did run well; who did hinder you that ye should not obey the truth?"*
>
> *- Galatians 5:7*

We want things to happen quickly; we want to live a life of comfort and peace. But we must remember that things that come quickly are only sometimes good.

In Biblical times, people would mainly run into battle and threats of danger. Today, we run for competitive races and to maintain our wealth. Despite this difference, we can still find inspiration from the Scripture when seeking motivation to run literally or figuratively. The race of life. Let this collection of Bible verses about running remind you of the importance of endurance and perseverance. God is with you and provides strength for the race ahead! He will never leave you behind, it's a distance run, and we must maintain a balance between being humbled and keeping that positive attitude, knowing He is the one running the race.

We can have the fruit we seek running the race and express that spiritual fruit's nature during challenging moments of the race! Where is this fruit, or what is it? Many Christians who believe in Christ asks me this question about "fruits" and the difference.

A 'fruit' is what a tree or plant bears of its kind that, when it lands on fertile ground, can reproduce more of its kind. And as we are the planting of the Lord, what kind of fruit do we bear? I share that if we are His children and not of the Devil's, and God is leading us to the vine, and we are the branches, we should bear the fruit of the Lord. I know we are fruit inspectors, and we should examine ourselves daily to ensure we are not waking up in the flesh. We have to remember who we are in Jesus' name!

"I am the true vine, and My Father is the vinedresser."

"Simple as that, and it's the only way to climb the ladder for stepping up to your responsibilities for salvation here. Branches can be broken, torn down, and mistreated by not obeying God's word. Every branch in me that does not bear fruit He takes away; and every branch that bears fruit He prunes, that it may bear more fruit. You are already clean because of the word I have spoken to you. Abide in Me, and I in you. As the branch cannot bear fruit of itself unless it abides in the vine, neither can you unless you abide in Me. I am the vine; you are the branches. He who abides in Me, and I in him, bears much fruit; for without Me you can do nothing."

These are Jesus' words of encouragement and compassion to us all.

"If anyone does not abide in Me, he is cast out as a branch and withered; they gather them and throw them into the fire, and they are burned. Who wants to be burned or left behind all this agony of not bearing good fruit? At first, I thought this was a ferry story or something out of this world I could not admit, genuine. If you abide in Me, and My words abide in you, you will ask what you desire, and it shall be done for you. By this My Father is glorified, that you bear much fruit; so you will be My disciples."

If He abides in us; if the Word of God abides in us. If we take in Christ and stay in the Word of God, and He abides in us, we will bear much fruit. This is the power of the Seed of God!

Jesus came to please the Father. And He glorified the Father, and He bore much fruit. Today, we are His extensions. The Father sent us the Holy Spirit to convict, save, lead and guide us and also to help us bear much fruit. In sharing the fruit of the Holy Spirit, by having Him flow through us, others can see and feel "Him" – the fruit of His ways, His love, and His personality... through the Holy Spirit in us, the body of Christ grows individually and corporately, in maturity and compassion!

This seems so difficult at times. There are days of relaxing, not reading God's word, and living your everyday life without any worries that I'm chosen or called to bear good fruit.

> *"...for whatever a man sows, that he will also reap. He who sows to his flesh will of the flesh reap corruption, but he who sows to the Spirit will of the Spirit reap everlasting life."*
>
> *– Galatians 6:7*

In the "world" we live in, there is a lot of "production," but not necessarily of the Lord.

This world is a "me, me, me" world. A "self-interested" and "self-serving" world... and its production does not "glorify the Father." The fruit from this setting is sensual, the "fruit of the flesh."

All of us bear some fruit.

The "Fruit of Our Carnal Nature" is the work of the flesh. But no matter what it's called, it is still fruit. Hate quickly gives birth to more hatred, bitterness, and bitterness. Thank God, when "the fruit of the Spirit is flowing," it is life-producing! When "works of the flesh" come against us and we return with "The Fruit of the Spirit," we open the door for God to work. When we honor our Father as Lord in our decisions and behavior, the fruit of His Spirit is "helping us" and "helping" those around us. Good choices glorify the Father and allow the Holy Spirit to work. This is the fruit of Christ in us. He works through His fruit! Ask yourself what kind of fruit you are putting out there as your example in walking the Christian lifestyle.

Whether someone is "sowing to the Spirit" or "sowing to the flesh," our actions affect others. Love is spiritual. Joy is spiritual. Kindness is spiritual. Spiritual things are not mystical. We are spiritual beings in physical housing. This is why when we "receive" hurt from something gone astray, we feel it in our hearts. We think with much more than our physical brain. The brain is physical. It is also spiritual when we send out a "hurt" to someone else. The physical and spiritual worlds are simultaneously happening all day, every day, but many people only realize the physical. We are blind by nature out of our mother's birth.

When Jesus said the Father wants us to worship Him in "spirit and in truth," He said it because He said that the Father wants sincerity and worship "truly from the heart." Things of the Spirit are just as real as things of the physical, only invisible. We see the evidence of where the Spirit goes, but we cannot see something of the Spirit. We are supposed to live life by faith and not by sight.

> *"For now, we see in a mirror dimly but then face to face. Now I know in part; then I shall know fully, even as I have been fully known."*
>
> *- 1 Corinthians 13:12*

Look at one of the verses in the Bible that talks about the fruit of the Spirit.

> *"But the fruit of the Spirit is love, joy, peace, patience, kindness, goodness, faithfulness, gentleness, and self-control; against such things, there is no law."*
>
> *- Galatians 5:22-23*

It's all genuine. As I write about these topics and explain their nature and power, it's essential to see the print as it's printed for your heart for wisdom and understanding!

> *"For the LORD gives wisdom; from His mouth come knowledge and understanding."*
>
> *- Proverbs 2:6*

Through God's words, we understand that God is the one who gives the gift of knowledge, that is, an understanding or awareness of something. The Lord, however, grants wisdom to those who have an honest relationship with him. I like giving insights into the value of knowledge and the path to gaining it. It has helped me grow in God's word and see nothing that dwells well in my flesh.

> *"For the desire of the flesh is against the Spirit, and the Spirit against the flesh; for these are in opposition to one another, to keep you from doing whatever you want."*

> *- Galatians 5:17*

These are good things that benefit everyone. When received or given, they bless. Consider the opposite. They do not build up or produce life. They take down your Spirit, feeling doomed and without the power of the Holy Spirit. Acts 1:8 tells us that Paul's charge to us was a warning and a reminder that we have an ability we can't neglect.

For all of us, "our actions" are "the fruit" of our choices. He is pure and good for the Holy Spirit and can only be good. Does it mean He does not hate evil or bring about brutal justice? He does whatever He does, from being good. And He wants us to do the same, making our decisions daily from the excellent place of our born-again spirits under the direction of the Holy Spirit. If we walk with Him daily as our Lord and Guide, our actions will be life-producing in blessing us; good choices empower us to feel we are headed to Heaven to work.

Look at some invisible, good attributes of the Spirit (Good Fruit.)

I wrote about these attributes because it's a crucial part of the Christian walk to notify the awakening of the body to produce these types of behavior and gifts in us:

Peacefulness, being joyful/happy, maturity, orderliness, purity friendliness, courtesy, encouragement, hope, loving, and thankful, amongst other things.

All these "fruits" enlighten us and those around us and give glory to God! Sometimes, we have to stand against corruption and horror, but even in those times, it is edifying. Take a stand against the Devil.

In contrast, look at some of these invisible bad attributes of the flesh (Bad Fruits):

Pride, harshness, cruelty, ungracious, unkindness, unrighteous anger, impatience, bitterness, rage, grudge-holding, record-keeping of wrongs, rude/quarrelsome, hateful, lovers of strife, discord, and hostility.

All these kinds of fruit should be informative for everyone. This fruit is "the works of the flesh" and is self-gratifying, hurtful, and destructive to the doer and recipients involved. Not only does this evil displease the Lord, but in choosing the such direction, it opens the door to empowering evil instead of good. Just as right choices empower God to work, wrong choices empower the dark side to work. Some people pray to God to work but end up encouraging the Devil to work by choosing unforgiveness and prejudice. Making wrong decisions (disobedience to God) enables the Devil to cause more hurt to others around us. We fall into his trap but disobey the Lord and disregard what He wants us to do: to be good to His creation.

We know that the Devil is the Father of lies and tricks. The Bible explains how he works in his craftiness.

The phrase "god of this world" (or "god of this age") indicates that Satan is a significant influence on the ideals, opinions, goals, hopes, and views of the majority of people. His power also encompasses the world's philosophies, education, and commerce. The thoughts, ideas, speculations, and false religions of the world are under his control and have sprung from his lies and deceptions. He is a deceiver and had us all fooled until we realized enough is enough. I know that without God and the fruits of the Spirit, I was lost and abandoned from my calling that I ignored for half of my life. Instead, I chose to do wrong and wanted what I desired best that was worst, in the end, to find myself crying out to God in a place of punishment. I wrote about it in 'Halftime Hustler,' my first book. I'm so happy I had awakened to God's Light to enlighten others about the deception I had fallen to. Being alive for Jesus is a relief of fresh gratification in my life. It was a tough road, but God had mercy on my heart and pulled me out of that web of lies. This is the difference between my current fruits and the previous ones I had produced.

The works (fruit) of the flesh are harmful, destructive, and addictive. Gratifying the evil nature is a never-ending cycle; the more it gets, the more it wants, and the sinful nature always wants more. What seems right to the worldly Spirit is always in direct conflict with the born-again spiritual nature. If the "evil nature" is allowed to "dominate," it will do its best to crush all that is good. It is destructive to the spirit person, but the damage and hurt do not stop there. In the long run, it is also harmful to the physical person. Bad habits are destructive to physical health all along the way of living.

Paul's statement in his first letter to the Corinthians, the apostle Paul wrote of the false teachers who had come into the Church at Corinth, teaching that the resurrection of Jesus Christ wasn't true. These people considered only their physical existence and denied life after death or the resurrection (**1 Corinthians 15:32**). Their moral outlook on life influenced the rest of the Corinthian believers. Bad company can be terrifying nowadays with the world we live in and follow! I enjoy discovering how we should follow Paul's warnings in this part of the Bible dealing with the Church and leaders before us.

Paul is telling us that by associating with false teachers, they will adversely influence us. The truth is that false teachings do not lead to holiness. As such, we must be careful whom we form relationships with, especially those outside the Church. Unbelievers can cause even the most righteous Christians to waver in their faith and adversely affect their walk with Christ and their witness to the world. This is why Paul tells us, "Do not be misled."

I find myself falling into my mind because I know some things I think or say are not spiritual. Yes, we sin and fight daily with our inner demons, but it is also wrong! The enemy is always around the corner or trying to convince us that we don't need to read about Paul's warnings.

This was the second time Paul warned the Corinthians not to be deceived (**1 Corinthians 6:9**). He cautioned them not to take up the lifestyles of corrupt people—those who will not inherit the kingdom of God. Paul knew how easy it is for people to be influenced by such adverse teachings. If not checked at the very beginning, they could adopt such perverted ideas and behaviors as the norm. For this reason, Paul tells us to stay awake and sober-minded because bad company corrupts good character. (**1 Corinthians 15:33**)

This is undoubtedly true because I have fallen into trouble hanging around a company that was influenced to lead me down the wrong path to darkness.

The point Paul makes here is pertinent to all people of all ages. When we associate with or delight in the company of people with worldly morals, we risk mimicking their behaviors, language, and habits. Before long, we are no longer of Christ but of the world with its denial of absolute authority, its rejection of the Bible as the Word of God, and its ideology of relative morality. This is especially pertinent to young people who are generally easily influenced by their peers. I have been there before and would not like to entertain these behaviors again. Young people are desperate for the approval of others. So motivated are they by the need for acceptance that godly wisdom in decision-making can go out the window in the face of peer pressure. Therefore, it is crucial for parents of young teens, especially, to be on guard against the influence of the wrong company.

So, what are we to do? Paul provides us with the answer at the very end of chapter 15:

> *"Therefore, my dear brothers, stand firm. Let nothing move you. Always give yourselves fully to the work of the Lord because you know that your labor in the Lord is not in vain."*

> *- 1 Corinthians 15:58*

As parents, we stand firm against ungodly influences that may corrupt our children. As Christians, we stand firm against those who would corrupt our walk with Christ. As church members, we stand firm against false teaching and watered-down gospel presentations that lead others astray. In all things, we are "self-controlled and alert" because our enemy, *"the Devil, prowls around like a roaring lion looking for someone to devour."* (**1 Peter 5:8**)

Worst of all, listening to evil (our carnal nature or the Devil) separates us from God and makes it harder and harder to hear His voice. There is no 'life' on that road while we are alive on earth or for all eternity.

The choices we make all day, every day, are essential. Sometimes we walk through life thinking everything is ok until it hits us right in the middle of the day with unexpected hardship! We ask ourselves, what just happened, and why is this happening in our life?

We can never get away from the things that are going to happen.

We can choose for good or bad. We can allow our Heavenly Father to lead us by His Spirit. He empowers us to do right. He knows when to turn and at what speed. Sometimes our choices have echoes far and wide. Why not let God be the faithful Lord and do like Jesus and live to please the Father? If we abide in Him and He in us, this is everything!

"If you abide in Me, and My words abide in you, you will ask what you desire, and it shall be done for you. By this My Father is glorified, that you bear much fruit; so you will be My disciples."

As we abide and grow in the Lord, we become more enlightened and continue in His plans for us. We have to study and join and serve in the Church. It's best to have good company because they will uplift you and encourage you in the faith.

We attain confidence in the ways of God. We learn to listen to the Holy Spirit and His guidance. Life will never be smooth sailing on this planet, but when Christ is the Captain, He knows how to take us through rough seas and calm them.

Most people move along through life without ever realizing the magnitude of their choices. They can harm us or make us, or break us!

Our Heavenly Father uses this "fruit synopsis" to help us be more aware of how life and death, good and evil, work in our lives. We, in general, are going forward, or we are going backward. There is no such thing as standing still. Every action we take, seen or unseen, is either life or death-producing. We can choose life and give the Father the honor and glory He deserves. We can be a blessing to others. The Lord can bear much fruit through us. Or we can choose poorly, gratifying the flesh, which dishonors God and gives the enemy tools to work with.

We can be the planting of the Lord, allowing Father God to bless us and others through the right choices. We can get forgiveness from the Lord for wrongdoing, but the echoes and hurts sometimes continue. Let our born-again spirits rule over our carnal natures and submit to the Holy Spirit. There is only goodness and life in choosing obedience to our Father. Let's abide in the Lord and have Him stay in us and glorify the Father. Let's go and bear much fruit by making life-producing, Heaven-empowering choices under the direction of the Holy Spirit!

CHAPTER 1: LOVE

"Whoever spares the rod hates their children, but the one who loves their children is careful to discipline them."

- Proverbs 13:24

Nowadays, the word "love" can be used in just about any context

"Do not love the world or anything in the world. If anyone loves the world, love for the Father is not in them."

- 1 John 2:15

Today, in our cultured world, we don't pay any attention to these verses. But the question people ask is, "Why should we?"

Well, I am a living example of how much you can give to the world and it will do nothing for you in return.

Here, write to your hearts what the world can do to you and give you nothing in return. It's like saving all your stuff to be treasured in your hearts.

Let's look at what holds us back and what true love is all about.

We "love" our families or soul mates, and we also "love" a good movie or pizza! It's no wonder people get so confused about the subject of love. The word "love" is just easy to say. Emotions and feelings get the best of us, and I think we need to look ideally at the meaning and content of this word the Bible speaks about.

One thing is sure: Every person on this earth was created with a deep longing to give and receive love. We develop our definition of love by how we were raised and what we saw modeled in our homes growing up. Whether we realize it or not, most people have a picture of God in their minds based on what their relationship was like with their earthly father. If their earthly father was kind and supportive, they would see God the same way. On the other hand, if their earthly father is unavailable or distant, they may find it difficult to see the unconditional love that God so freely gives. My father was never around, and I resent him for leaving my mother and being far away from me as his son. It felt distant in my heart because all my high school friends had their fathers around, and I used to call my best friend's Dad "Pops" because he was always there for me. He was there during the basketball high school season games, along with his son, of course, who had a real father there to watch the games. Sometimes, we feel we dealt the short end of the stick and feel left out.

I grew up in a home where "I love you" was as natural as "hello." To this day, if you are around my family for a very long, you will hear those three little words because we look for opportunities to express our love for one another. I realize that it's easy for me to accept God's love because of how I was raised, but maybe you weren't raised in a family like mine, and it's hard for you to believe God is so loving and forgiving. If so, maybe it's time for you to "redefine" what you know as love. My mother showed tough love, and I often remember her saying, "Boy, I love you, and I will still wring your neck if you keep it up!"

God's love goes way beyond any human love you've ever experienced! He is always patient and kind, always just and forgiving.

He weeps when you weep and laughs when you laugh. You are His delight, and He longs to have a loving, tender relationship with you. You bring joy to His heart, and I know He is smiling at you as you read these words. This did not mean my mother did not love me or followed God and mistreated us all growing up. It was her way of expressing her emotions, and establishing discipline in the house.

I want you to know today that God is not mad at you; He loves you! It doesn't matter how many times you've made a mistake; it doesn't matter how many times you've blown it; God is always ready to receive you with open, loving arms. Can you imagine God in front of you with

His arms outstretched, ready to welcome you? Don't run away from Him; run toward Him. Simply take a step of faith to embrace His love and forgiveness.

If you've never accepted the love and forgiveness that Jesus has to offer, let me encourage you to do so right now! I'm not talking about becoming religious and trying to be good enough; I'm talking about having a personal, loving relationship with the Creator of the universe through His Son, Jesus.

It can be challenging to grab hold of his cross and fill like you can do 100 pull-ups, and that's all it takes! It's like time and growth that makes the seed mature. Do 11 pull-ups and walk humbled, and watch Jesus bless you in this love of power he is trying to show us with strength.

"Love thy neighbor" is a significant Bible verse I always remember in the faith that may appear as a quick remark but actually holds significant meaning to my faith. Being kind and loving towards those around you, whether a partner, family member, friend or neighbor, is true to your faith. You can show your love for that special someone or important figure in a million different ways, but if they are also Christian, sharing one of the following Bible verses about love may be the perfect gesture. Yes, it's hard to love at all times and follow the way Jesus teaches us in the word of God. I find it challenging to love those who don't love me back. Do I love my enemies or those who try to trap me or harm my family? These are questions I asked myself when I read in the Bible how we as Christians are supposed to handle that direction to take!

There are so many passages in the Bible that speak to the theme of love. Finding a relevant passage to share or reading yourself can be overwhelming if you are looking for some reflection and information. Luckily, I have come across a lovely collection of verses that describe the importance of loving others as God has loved us and relate to specific relationships you may have. Every day of the year is a great day to read one of these Bible verses about love to the people you care about most and recite group prayers with those who may need a little bit of love in their life right now. We all need love to think of it or not! We all want to be respected and never stepped on or treated as bad, right? Of course not! I hated being treated as an outcast or the last to be noticed or honored, even though I had tried hard to win something.

There are endless ways to express your love for one another. For some, showing love means taking out the trash on a freezing night, so your loved one doesn't have to do it themselves. For others, love is expressed more directly by reciting bedtime stories or outright saying, "I love you." And for those who believe in God and follow the teachings of Jesus Christ, love takes on a whole new meaning. The best Bible verses about God's love prove that even in your darkest hours, when it may seem like you're on your own, or that you lost everyone and everything you've ever cared about; He is always there, and you are never alone.

Have you ever felt a dark moment or week, month, or year of darkness and can't seem to find your way out? Of course, we all have been there, and I know I have faced many dark tunnels. I even had to crawl through them all alone but not alone!

I have felt this 'abandoned' feeling, in danger and, of course, in trouble with the law. I was unsaved and blind to God's love for my direction and salvation.

God's immense and unwavering love isn't always easy to see or understand. Sometimes it shows itself in small ways, like when a person asks how your day is going and listens when you answer. It also shows itself in significant ways, like when a guardian angel appears out of nowhere when your car stops running, and you need someone to restart it. Bible verses about God's love are a constant reminder that He is always watching and ready to help, and they'll allow you to take comfort in the fact that He is always in your corner. Does that sound familiar, or have you expected God to just show up, and it seems he is not there? I was in court years back and will never forget that even though the number of witnesses all stood in the courthouse lobby, I knew I was guilty because the judge would see the credibility of the witnesses and find me guilty, right? Well, we know God is in Control, and after being found guilty and paying the penalty for my choices, it was the best thing that could of happen for my faith in Jesus. So, to me, he did show up and was always there for me through those tuff times of facing my mistakes into facing solid faith.

In **Matthew 17:20**, I read a verse to remind me of this moment that was happening. It's mind bubbling when you sense something strange around you is going on, right? That day was beautiful, even though it was the most fearful day in my sight. Faith is the substance of things not seen, and we hope to see them down the road ….

> *"Because of your little faith. For truly, I say to you, if you have faith like a grain of mustard seed, you will say to this mountain, 'Move from here to there,' and it will move, and nothing will be impossible for you."*

– Matthew 17:20

Love Originates in God

The first and most important thing we must recognize about love is that it's all about God. In **John 17**, what's sometimes called the "High Priestly Prayer," Jesus prays for Christians, both present and future. He asks the Father to grant his people unity and love, and he will keep us until the end amid the world's inevitable hatred.

Jesus also prays for himself, specifically about his imminent death: *"Father, the hour has come. Glorify your Son, that your Son may glorify you."*

A few verses later, he continues: *"Father, I want those you have given me to be with me where I am and to see my glory, the glory you have given me because you loved me before the creation of the world."*

I see this as "tough love" and sacrifice because to even think the way Jesus did on the cross in so much pain, having his mind on his Father and not himself. When we go through pain or much suffering that is hard to bare or deal with for so long, we get weak and think of ourselves and how to stop the pain, right?

Just pause for a second.

Imagine you didn't exist. In fact, imagine nothing had ever existed— no people, no places, no things, no pain or suffering!

Is anything left?

According to Jesus, there is. There's love. The love between the eternally loving, eternally secure, and always complete Godhead.

Without the Father loving the Son and the Spirit, the Son loving the Father and the Spirit, and the Spirit loves the Father and the Son—all "before the creation of the world"—we would know nothing of love because love would have never existed.

So what must we say about love? We must begin where the Bible begins, and the Bible finds the foundation of love in the Trinity.

I will quote this verse again and again.

> *"For God so loved the world, that he gave his only begotten Son, that whosoever believeth in him should not perish, but have everlasting life."*
>
> *- John 3:16*

How did God show His love for us? By sacrificing his Son for our eternal good on a cross.

In the Scripture, love is entwined with substitutionary sacrifice. We find this connection's real in the death and resurrection of Christ, the Perfect One who died and rose again, victorious. The cross is proof of the Son's sacrifice; the empty tomb is proof of the Father's acceptance of that sacrifice. Both together display God's love.

Yes, it's hard for some of us to understand.

The truth of the Scripture is vertical, meaning it primarily deals with the relationship between God and man, Creator and the creation. Often, however, God clarifies the vertical via the horizontal, using horizontal imperatives—"Do this"—as a test for the presence of sheer realities.

So it is with love. Just as God's love for us in Christ was sacrificial, so should our love be for each other.

"By this everyone will know that you are my disciples if you love one another."

- John 13:35

The same is true of Paul at the outset, where he connects the Christian ethic of love to the sacrifice of Christ. "Agreeing" and "having the same love" leads us to the same person: Jesus Christ. He has set the example; he is our road map toward love and humility. The puzzle is simple: God loved us sacrificially in Christ; therefore, we love others.

It's also important to note that "Greater love has no one than this: to lay down one's life for one's friends" is immediately followed by *"You are my friends if you do what I command."*

Jesus's clarification introduces an element of authority into the definition of love. This clarification grates against our culture and our desire for self-rule, even as Christians, not-yet-glorified. But this contrast must be stressed because any definition of love with no room for authority is simply sub-biblical.

Having a relationship with God means submitting ourselves to his lordship under his excellent authority. We don't become Christians, so we can run up a massive debt on the sin card and expect Daddy to bail us out. It doesn't work that way.

Instead, our disposition toward sin and holiness changes. We switch teams because we're no longer committed to our own choices. We're now united to Christ by faith, so what is his by merit is now ours by grace. This is Paul's point in **Romans 6**: *"What shall we say, then? Shall we go on sinning so that grace may increase? 2 By no means!"*

Why? Because we've died to sin and are now slaves of God.

It's impossible to "love" Christ while clinging to our unfettered freedom. This setup is to desire a mirage, a trick of the Devil. All of us are under the authority of some master. It's merely a question of whether that master is harsh, fickle, and impossible to please (like sin) or gracious, constant, and pleased by trust (like God). Our King loves us by enabling us to live under his rule.

In the past, I used to be very fickle and could not make my mind up to live for God the way he wanted me to accept him. It was always a road in front of me yelling at me to walk this way, and even though it seemed shorter or delightful, I would find myself serving the wrong master.

> *"No one can serve two masters, for either he will hate the one and love the other; or else he will be devoted to one and despise the other."*
>
> *Matthew 6:24*

Finally, love looks toward Heaven. It doesn't just have the "now" in mind. This manifests itself in at least two ways.

First, Christians love by reminding one another of their unchangeable status in Christ and pointing to the cross, the empty tomb, and Jesus's promised return.

Second, because conversion is genuine and Christians are "new creations," when the occasion requires, they love by reminding each other of the seriousness of sin and, with God's help, push each other toward holiness. This is why it's almost always from a place of love—not judgment or nosiness—when a brother or sister-in-Christ confronts us regarding our sin, even if the delivery leaves something to be desired. Though it may wound our pride, bristle our self-surety, and tempt an argumentative response, deep down, we should know it comes from a place of kindness intended by God for our good.

These confrontations can be tricky, especially when they test our relationships with non-Christians or those who claim to be Christians but, by all accounts, appear self-deceived.

And yet, even in these situations, love looks toward Heaven. Christians love non-Christians with "Heavenward" love by warning them of their eternal state, commending the gospel, and holding out Jesus as Savior. If non-Christians were to read this article, I hope they'd find it as forthright and engaging as it is disconcerting and confrontational.

Similarly, speaking Christians love professing Christians mired in unrepentant sin by calling them to hold fast both to Christ and the substance of their profession. Based on their response, we either rejoice in their repentance or continue the process laid out for us in **Matthew 18** and **1 Corinthians 5:** In the regrettable occasions when a professing believer persists in his or her sin, Christians love by excluding him or her from their number "so that their spirit may be saved on the day of the Lord." Even this—church discipline, as it's often called—is an act of heavenward love.

The world always says love is love. But the God of the Bible—not us—tells us what this self-referential sentence actually means.

He tells us of love's origin—that love is essentially riveted outside ourselves to the nature and character of the triune God. Second, he shows us his love in the sacrifice of his Son: a love that is both gracious because it is contra-conditional and authoritative because it changes us, bestowing on us through the Spirit the very things it requires. Finally, the Bible's definition of love varies in how we love others— believers, non-believers, and professing believers stuck in sin.

The Bible says a lot about love but raises expectations and changes us. It paints an ocean while the world splashes around in a puddle. It's almost as if love is at your front door waiting to come in. It's always reaching out to us and trying to get our attention.

Mable is at her last end with her daughter. She's ready to dish out some tough love. Biff's teen has broken curfew again. He says it's time for a little tough love. Bart is frustrated with his friend.

"It's time for some tough love action," he says. May I have a dollar for every time I have heard the tough love mantra attached to these tones? In these contexts, folks play and misapply the "tough love card."

Since the Bible does not say or mention tough love, it would be best to start with a Biblical framework here, right? Words like mercy, kindness, or grace better frame your goals for corrective care. These are the words that I typically attach to the discipleship life coach leadership process. For example, when I counsel a couple where sin has captured one of the spouses (**Galatians 6:1**), I might say it was "a mercy from the Lord that has interrupted your plans and brought you to this place of change."

I talk about how kind and Loving God is to intervene in their lives to stop them from sinning and to get help. These words apply to any person captured by sin. Though he may feel like "tough things" are happening to him, you want to ensure that he sees what is happening through mercy, kindness, and grace.

The Givers – How you think about a concept will set the stage for responding to others. I like how Paul talked about tough love in **Romans 2:4**. He used the word "kindness," which means "loving-kindness." It is the loving-kindness of God that brings change to someone. If you want to help someone change, try loving kindness. Let's reframe our three frustrated friend's struggles.

- Mable is at her last end with her daughter. She's ready to dish out some loving-kindness.
- Jerry's teen has broken curfew again. He says it's time for a bit of loving-kindness.
- Bart is frustrated with his friend. "It's time for some loving-kindness action," he says.

The Receivers: I was counseling someone years ago, and he said I was mean. I asked him what he meant by the word *mean*. He told someone who had warned him before he met me that I would get deep into his heart. I replied, "Did your friend say I was mean?" The counselee said, "No, that was my word, not theirs. They said it would get rough because you would get into my heart."

The counselee saw getting into his heart as being mean, which showed his interpretation of what was about to happen. He was afraid of the counseling process.

As he drove to the office, my fearful counselee even talked himself into being scared. He expected the worst and prepared accordingly; he entered the session in a defensive posture. He was expecting tough love, not mercy, kindness, and grace. If you believe the change process will be challenging, dear, you will get what you expect.

Whether you're giving or receiving corrective care, your presupposition sets your mind and guides your actions for the experience. It would be best to think about any discipleship opportunity as the Lord doing redemptive work. Attributing adverse connotations to redemptive purposes is not wise.

Any transformative action in a person will be challenging, but the guarantee is that if you're willing to root out the sin, you will experience God's mercy and grace.

I do not see God's intervention in my life as tough love. I see it as His mercy. To think Creator God would slow down long enough to think about my act upon me and motivate me to change is stunning. Oh, my soul. I can hardly bear the thought. God loves you if you are His. You should not be afraid of Him. He does not use tough love but merciful, gracious, loving-kindness.

While I want to be cautious about how I speak for Him, I don't believe He wants His children to think about Him as tough. I'm a parent too. I don't want my children to feel that way about me. I hope they will remember me for mercy, grace, and love, not more authoritarian disciplinary actions, even though I have not withheld firm, corrective care.

Too often, when someone talks about tough love, they are speaking from a frustrated heart. Like Mable, Jerry and Bart, they have had enough of their family and friends, and it is time to react to them in a complex manner that would change them.

Strong, directive care is proper if it is born out of a heart that produces compassion, mercy, grace, and love for the person they are helping. The Lord chastens the one He loves (**Hebrews 12:6** "If you love the ones you chasten, you should expect these three things in this order").

- Mercy and grace will control your heart.
- Mercy and grace will season your speech.
- Mercy and grace will affect the person you're helping.

What's your view on God?

As an illustration of these ideas, I have appealed to my small group members about how they talk about the depth and degree to which we speak of holding each other accountable within the group. I use wisdom to communicate about what happens in our small groups. There is a temptation for some people to leave the small group by saying something along these lines.

I hold Bible studies with 7 other men, and we always seem to have a way of correcting one another in love, at least most of the time. When I'm in a youth life coach moment speaking to youth - it's different because the mind has not developed yet, and it's a more significant fight to pick up the cross and follow Jesus right!

We had a great group tonight. We pulled out the two-by-fours and got after it, talking about sin. God stepped all over our toes. [Small group member] brought his A-game. There was grace in this place, and so awesome.

This retelling of a small group night does not communicate the Grace and mercy of God. It is an unwise speech that can cause a brother or sister to stumble. It would be better not to talk about tough love in hyperbolic ways but to use the biblical language of mercy, grace, and love. The small group member could speak to their friends like this:

We met God in our small group. He was so gracious to us. Some things were going on in my life, and [small group member] loved me enough to address them. My wife was blessed. It edified our group. God's fame was made even more fabulous. I experienced mercy from the Lord.

This retelling is more accurate and gives you a better view of who God is and how He cares for us, plus His diligence in our lives. Knowing how to think about love and communicate its effects on others is vital.

Words Define God

Part of the problem with discussing discipline is our weak understanding of God. For example, if things go the way we want, we believe God is good. "Yay! God came through for me." We think of God as complicated and difficult if things do not go how we want. We define God by how our life goes. God is merciful, kind, and gracious all the time. That's it.

As you work through the character traits of God, there is no trait called the hash. As His children, we are supposed to imitate Him.

Therefore, we aim not to be tough on others but merciful, kind, and gracious, even when we suffer hard things.

- When God confronts you, what do you feel most, the love of God or the toughness of God?
- When called out for your sin, do you see it as God's mercy working in your life?
- When a brother or sister confronts you for a legitimate issue, do you see it mainly as God's mercy or that person being tough on you?

How you answer these questions reveals where you are with the "tough love problem" and your application of God's mercy and His Grace. Your thoughts reveal your practical theology. Even if someone is mean telling you the truth! Your heart is in the right place with God, and you will find God's Grace and mercy, even though it was an imperfect presentation. (I'm not speaking of abusive situations but of someone who genuinely loves you and wants the best for you.)

Tough love could be challenging to get your head around, but when you think about loving-kindness, merciful actions, or grace-filled interventions, your mind will adjust, and you can proceed biblically. It's always a practice and study of reading your Bible and growing into the word as if you are in it and running the race with it.

"Loving unconditionally."

It's easy to love people that are just like us: people that look like us, dress like us and worship like us. That doesn't take a lot of effort. But what about people that are different than us, people that we don't understand or agree with?

As far as we're concerned, they're making poor choices. It's easy to size them up from the exterior, put them in a box, and think they're not for me; they're odd. I'm going to keep my distance. But God's love is not exclusive; it's inclusive. It doesn't exclude people that are different. It doesn't write people off because they're not where they should be. It recognizes someone because they need to meet our standards.

Unconditional love says I'm going to love you even if I disagree with you. I may disagree with your lifestyle, your doctrine, how you're raising your children, and the friends you're choosing, but I know this. You are made in the image of almighty God, and I am not called to judge you. I am called to love you, and we must realize every person is on a journey.

Where they are right now is different from where they will end up. They're not finished; they're still on the potter's wheel. God is working with all of us; no one is perfect or without completion. We all have fallen short of his glory.

Sometimes I feel alone and without all my family's or anyone's support! We all like to feel supported and loved. We usually suspect family members to love us no matter what or be there for us and have the opportunity to run to them or call them or be there when life seems overwhelming.

It is very noticeable that people's love has grown cold, and they have difficulty choosing between the world and the Spirit of God. (Matthew 6:24) it's all around us, and you can see it daily.

"No one can serve two masters, for either he will hate the one and love the other; or else he will be devoted to one and despise the other."

I hope this topic is crucial in my eyes and other believers! This made me fall from my true calling, materialistic ways of walking in this world. Now that this is behind me and I can share the thoughts of how blind I was with these things that were deceiving me, hopefully, it will encourage others to see that those things are not as important as your salvation or peace of mind.

We live in materialistic times. The tendency all around us is to acquire money and material possessions. Materialism and consumerism are the primary engines of human action. As a result, we apply an economic outlook to all areas of life. 'Does this decision benefit me monetarily?' 'Does that action limit me materially?' These are questions we ask about all aspects of life. I used to think, *God, what happened to me, and why don't I have those things that my neighbor has? Why do I not have these things when I worked so hard and saved so much money?*

Those who work in the financial sector of society encounter this to an even greater extent. But this tendency does not escape any social class. Those who have little often concern themselves with how they can obtain more. The same goes for those who belong to the middle class of society. The wealthy and prosperous continue to concern themselves with wealth, mainly how they may preserve it, increase it, and spend it.

Moreover, this is not just the prevailing attitude during prosperous economic times. Currently, some see a recession on the horizon. It is possible that this prospect only increases our preoccupation with possessions. Some will concentrate on salvaging whatever they can recover. Others will exert themselves even more. Still, others will become more fearful, and that fear will enslave them all the more to materialism.

We sometimes just don't know why we do what we do because the flesh is always tempted, and the mind is willing to follow. Paul's statement about these lustful things is carnal and not suitable to lust after.

> *"Do not store up for yourselves treasures on earth, where moths and vermin destroy, and where thieves break in and steal. 20 But store up for yourselves treasures in heaven, where moths and vermin do not destroy, and where thieves do not break in and steal. 21 For where your treasure is, there your heart will be also."*
>
> *- Matthew 6:19-21*

Clearly, this attitude leads to viewing life in terms of material things. Our focus will be on the things we see, hear, and touch, not the things of God and spiritual life; not on repentance and humbly walking before God; not on being an imitator of Christ. Such a materialistic outlook on life, which idolizes the material, stands in direct opposition to the calling of Christian discipleship.

There is only one weapon against such an outlook: to turn away from this focus and turn to the living God again and again. We must grow spiritually by becoming stewards of our earthly possessions and strangers. I had to focus on reading daily just to keep my heart pumping with Jesus and his direction for my life. What a reminder in **Romans 12:2**:

> *"Do not conform to the pattern of this world, but be transformed by the renewing of your mind. Then you will be able to test and approve what God's will is—His good,*

pleasing and perfect will."

This Bible verse reminds me that I need to stay clear of being absent from this very thing. I know God directs my mind to his glory if I read his word and stay clear of danger.

Of course, the concept here is fundamental.

The Bible offers a God-centered view of material possessions. First of all, we have been created as image bearers of God. That is a high position and a high calling. God has entrusted His creation to us and commanded us to dress and to keep it to till the ground and to tend, work and care for God's creation.

We are to observe the boundaries of creation and not overstep the limits set by God. The Bible says that we are created in his image and should remember Genesis, the first chapter about cultivating the earth and producing good fruits.

The mandate to till the ground and cultivate the earth has been given to man as an image bearer of God. Man is to cultivate because he bears God's image. Animals are not the image-bearers of God and have not received this mandate. Man alone has acquired the cultural mandate.

In performing this task, we must comply with God's Laws.

We must provide for our own livelihood. If any will not work, neither let him eat. The point is that if any refuses to work, let him go hungry. It does not mean that if any cannot work or can no longer work, let him go hungry. On the contrary, our hearts should go out to those in real need. Nevertheless, we must provide for our livelihood. We are responsible for our subsistence and sustenance.

The framework of this stewardship is love for God and our neighbor. Our work is never meant to profit ourselves only, not even only God, but also for the benefit of serving and helping our fellow man. That is how God ordained it. God calls us to have dominion as stewards under Him.

That is not the same as being autonomous or independent owners. On the contrary, stewardship under Him means that we govern God's creation while depending on Him and realizing that we are accountable to the chief Owner, the Lord our God. We may manage, use and enjoy His gifts, but always the awareness that God asks us to give an account of how we operate, use and enjoy them.

Since Man's fall (**Genesis 3:1**) sin has been a disrupting and destructive force. We see this in three ways:

- It severs the harmonious relationship with God.
- It violates the good use of God's gifts.
- We no longer see God as the Giver, the Source, and the Object of His good gifts. We deprive our fellow man of our service. Instead, we make excessive use of God's gifts, or we covet these gifts for ourselves only.

Because of sin, we no longer regard ourselves as stewards accountable to God and dependent upon Him. Instead, we fancy ourselves to be lords and masters, whereas we actually are slaves. We do not possess them as gifts from God, but they possess us. Think of the Lord Jesus' warning not to store up for oneself treasures on earth, where moth and rust destroy, and where thieves break in and steal (**Matthew 6:3**). James writes in the same way in the Bible;

Today we may have other forms of "gold" and "silver," but their temptations are equally strong, and their rewards similarly destructive.

What does life delivered from slavery look like? A redeemed life continues to be a broken life. Yet, it focuses on the future. When we turn to God from idols to serve the living and true God, we also wait for His Son from Heaven. They are provisions on the way. As stewards, we use them, always looking forward, forgetting what is behind.

> *"I press on to reach the end of the race and receive the heavenly prize for which God, through Christ Jesus, is calling us."*
>
> *– Phil 3:14*

Far as I am concerned, we are never totally at home here on earth. We are strangers because we belong to the kingdom of Heaven (**Phil 3:20**). Our citizenship is in Heaven. It is true that our flesh and the world oppose us and seek to hinder us; therefore, we must resist the temptations to continue as slaves of money and possessions. These things can seriously detour your walk in Christ a step backward, as if you had the Devil come under your feet and tripped you up to fall hard. This was my issue for sure thinking that it's a way to feel or be successful because of the things of the world. That really had taken a role in deceiving my directions for sure!

As we battle, we await the final triumph. At times we may rest a little. We call these times "oases," places of refreshment in the desert.

Boy, I felt like it was a complete desert of pain sitting in a place far away from home, wondering when or if I ever make it out of this place.

Being incarcerated was the worst but the best because I had turned from the darkness and returned to the light of who I really am. It was a time to click with Jesus and stay focused on what was important in my growth during an isolation period.

A proper estimate of the Lord's Day is important to me! It has been given to us with the command to worship God in a particular way. It is not just a day for recreation. The Lord's s day is a day of spiritual reflection to reflect on the present and the future.

Strengthened by that rest, we continue to do battle. Do we experience the Lord's Day this way? A great deal in our lives still needs to be changed. True conversion also influences the way we spend the Lord's Day. Let us spend the Lord's Day in the tension of the vigilance of being a "sentry post" focusing on the end of the pilgrimage. We must defend our Sunday as a day of rest. This means that we must take heed to attend the worship services as well as to our spiritual well-being.

This warning needs to be sounded: Secularism is taking the day of rest from us. The Christian who properly regards the Lord's Day will not be imprisoned by money nor obsessively cling to it. Instead, moderation will be our watchword.

The Christian life is a life of *thankfulness*. The Christian sees God as the Giver, Who determines the boundaries we must respect. It is also a life of *sharing*.

We do not just receive our possessions for ourselves but also to share them with others. To what extent should this sharing be done?

This depends, in part, on your situation, the circumstances of your life, and your age. I have been using tithing as a guideline. This applies not only to our money but also to our time. Christians should ask how they might spend this time to the advantage of the church or various ministries. To give is enriching, and it gives joy. Those who do not find joy in passing; I exhort you to seriously and sincerely examine yourself at this point. Thankfully, you had a better question about whether you know what it is to receive from the Lord and what it is to give.

Paul pleads with the Corinthians to have the attitude of possessing as though not possessing (**1 Corinth 30:7**). We may use and enjoy the possessions that the Lord entrusts to us, but we may not set our hearts on them (**cf. Ps. 62:1-3**)

God richly provides us with everything for our enjoyment. At the same time, Timothy charges them that they become *"rich in good works, ready to distribute, willing to communicate."*

That is, we are to share with others what we have received. We must and may lovingly do something and resist the temptation. You are not to gather everything for yourself but rather use it for God and your neighbor. Then you are building on a good foundation for the future!

It takes work to understand. Let me restate it as follows:

> *"After you have suffered for a little while, the God of all grace, who called you to His eternal glory in Christ, will Himself perfect, confirm, strengthen, and establish you."*
>
> *- 1 Peter 5:10*

There is no merit on our part that God rewards. Instead, it is by grace that we build on Christ as the foundation. Sharing with others what we have received gives evidence that Christ governs us.

In that way, we have a perspective on eternal life. To sum it up, such an attitude of sharing what we have received with others indicates that faith is active, living, and lively. This is God's Grace!

CHAPTER 2: JOY

"Consider it pure joy, my brothers and sisters, whenever you face trials of many kinds, because you know that the testing of your faith produces perseverance. Let perseverance finish its work so that you may be mature and complete, not lacking anything."

- James 1:2-4

Everyone wants to experience joy, but most people don't know where to find it. Fortunately, the Scripture provides countless verses that can help you find your place of happiness, regardless of your circumstances.

There was a time in my own life when I needed to realize that I needed happiness to feel truly blessed. But happiness comes from God and not from the world around us.

I want to share my experience of walking into pure bliss and being called by God. I have read a lot of Bible verses and have taken numerous steps to ensure there is peace and happiness in my life. Reading them will encourage and motivate you to reach out to God, no matter how difficult your circumstances are.

One of the most powerful ways to find joy in the Lord is through prayer and worship. The Bible instructs us to "Rejoice in the Lord." As we praise God in worship, our hearts are filled with joy. As you worship God, ask Him to fill you with His Spirit. This is what I have trained myself to do every day to ensure there is joy in my life.

"May the God of hope fill you with all joy and peace as you trust in him, so that you may overflow with hope by the power of the Holy Spirit."

- Romans 15:13

Jesus is the perfect example of not giving up, and giving in to the Devil and his tricks. We all face different trials and suffering in moments of temptation. I get it, and understand that the heat of the moment, and pressure of fighting for this joy, to shine in my own personal lifestyle has been a struggle! *Yes*, it has been for a long time, and the race is still ongoing, but God is the one leading me to victory.

My flesh does not want to obey at times and follow His directions. It's so frustrating when I find myself confused or double-minded when it comes to making decisions.

When I was writing this chapter, I kept wondering about what I should share and I thought of.

As I have pondered what I might share in this chapter of Joy I, kept reverting back to the second half of **Nephi 2:25**: *"Adam fell that men might be; and men are, that they might have joy."*

If you ask me, it's an amazing verse that is thought-provoking. Without joy, it's impossible to be happy and enjoy life. It's part of the Holy Spirit to have it and walk with it!

Sometimes, I feel empty when I'm not following the word of the Lord. I don't feel any happiness and joy in my life. I feel disconnected from the world and myself.

We're all humans and we all struggle, cry, feel frustrated, and depressed sometimes. Being able to hold onto the feelings of joy is an experience unlike any other. There are days I feel regret, and days I feel secure through the joy that comes with speaking about the word of God.

"It shall blossom abundantly, and rejoice even with joy and singing."

- Isaiah 35:2

This has long been one of my favorite scriptures, firstly, because it is short. As a teenager going to public schools and being raised in a huge family, I really struggled to memorize any scripture. My older brother went to seminary and was the great "Scripture Mastery Guy" who memorized things and knew where to find stuff.

I had a terrible time; I couldn't remember things, so that was one scripture I really enjoyed but forgotten to write it down while growing up.

Basketball was a big deal in my life as a teenager attending high school. Secondly, because I was a young man growing up, not being a member of any church, I always thought life was supposed to be fun and games. To me, joy equated to happiness, which meant doing things I liked. This meant having fun.

The Church, and attending Church, was supposed to be fun! I was always invited by a friend whose parents were religious.

As I reflect on the past 49 years on what joy or happiness has looked like to me, it is clear that my interpretation of 'joy' and what has brought me happiness in this life has changed somewhat through the various stages of my life. I had to face many tests; and I know for a fact that I will face more challenges in the future because the hustle never stops!

With this thought in my mind as I attended different churches, I was surprised by the number of times the word "joy" was used in the Testimony. It stuck out to me, from pastors who spoken on that topic! It was re-impressed upon my mind that our God—my Father and your Father in Heaven—He who has all power, really, *really*, wants us to be happy. I just could not understand this as a youth or teen in college. For some reason, I knew it was something I needed whilst growing up because I know it's key to our spiritual survival.

Lehi had been persecuted, left all his possessions, and fled Jerusalem into the wilderness, and was living in a tent.

Clearly, Lehi knew opposition, anxiety, heartache, pain, disappointment, and sorrow. Yet, he declared boldly and without reservation, a principle as revealed by the Lord: *"**And men are, that they might have joy.**"*

Imagine! Of all the words he could have used to describe the nature and purpose of our lives here in mortality, he chose the word "joy"!

Like I said, this word is something unique and a gift from God. I thought I had it a few years back but it reappeared when I needed it most. Now that I have the Joy of the Lord, it's made a significant difference in my life that I was never able to see before.

I have also realized the joy we feel has little to do with the *circumstances* of our lives and everything to do with the *focus* of our lives. When the focus of our lives is on God's plan of salvation, Jesus Christ, and His gospel, we can feel joy regardless of what is happening, or not happening in our lives. Joy comes from Him. He is the source of all joy.

I did not understand this until I had to suffer a great test of isolation in my life that created a determination to find happiness and bliss, and improve myself as an individual!

> *"The heart is deceitful above all things, and desperately sick; who can understand it?"*
>
> *- Jeremiah 17:9*

Yes, of course, joy is also in the heart and out of the heart flows the fountain of life. But God knows our mind, heart, and character! We have to hear His voice and not stumble against the fence trying to pick which side to relax on.

It's not always easier said than done. Can we live fulfilling lives without money, status, glitz, and glamor? I believe that the only way to seek joy in life is to follow the Lord and His calling.

The spiritual principle that the very reason we exist is to have joy can fill each of us with hope, faith, and knowledge that a bigger, better, brighter future is awaiting us, made possible by our Faith in God. Some of us go without this faith in God or reading the words of the Bible to bring joy out of the pages and into our lives.

Joy is a gift for the Faithful. It comes from intentionally trying to live a righteous life, as taught by Jesus Christ. We know it's all a part of the Fruit of the Spirit.

With that in mind, I have five principles from the experiences in my life that have helped me recognize where my joy is and has been found. I thought things, places, and adventures gave me real joy! Also, particularly in mind: parties, clubs, women, material things, and friends. Well, those things and behaviors landed me in an even worse place where I was left alone to pick up the pieces!

I was deceived once again in many ways of how something was nothing but a dead-end to joy, and that blinded me. How was I going to get myself out of this can of worms that had me trapped in a box of closed doors for a period of many years?

I asked myself such questions because it was painful to explain my suffering. I thought could I ever be happy and enjoy life like everyone else that seemed at peace and completely put together. I looked through a dirty glass one day and saw others' lives as dirty inside, but the outside was clean. That's how I felt before getting into trouble with the law and making terrible mistakes that landed me with the can of worms. Jesus told me over time that we can't serve two masters and we can't pick both of them. I was always straddling the fence and trying to choose both of them.

> *"You blind Pharisee, first clean the inside of the cup and of the dish, so that the outside of it may also become clean."*
>
> *- Matthew 23:26*

The craziest thing about all of this is that I thought I had a great life to get back to but it was even better letting God put me through what He had to, in order for me to see what He had planned for me. He took me away from a life of shadows and regrets, and filled my world with joy.

Now, I think about what my life was like before Him. Do I really want that kind of life again? Would I be better off set free from what I was facing?

These are questions we all need to ask ourselves when we lose something worth better and joyful. We can't see it until it happens and that's when the faith should be taking over, not our idea of what faith should be!

Jesus said that we have to be real with ourselves and choose Him rather than ourselves!

Well, it's easier said than done. Life is about choices and we seem to pick what we know, or have been taught growing up.

We hear about it in primary when we sing, "I am a Child of God."

We read about it in the scriptures as God addresses Moses and states, "thou art my son."

When we understand who we are and what our potential is, we gain perspective that lifts us up and enables us. I believe each of us experiences in our lives moments where God reaches out, to help us understand that perspective, just as he did for Moses. He wants each of us to know who we are.

For me, this first occurred through an experience I had as a young boy when my mom asked me to go and pick up a loaf of bread from the dairy. Now a 'dairy' in Compton is a small convenience store; think 7-Eleven but smaller. Well, it was the store that was just under half a mile from our house, and my mom gave me $10to go get bread and milk. This felt like a lot of money to entrust a nine year old boy with!

A pint of milk was only 125 cents at the time and a loaf of bread, about 89 cents. I'm not sure why, but I can only imagine it was because I was young, and I *could*, I ran up the hill over the road, and down the street to the dairy as fast as I could.

When I was almost there, I tripped and tumbled to the ground. As I gathered myself, I realized in a panic that the change from buying the items which I had been holding tightly and safely in my hand was no longer there. I immediately began searching the ground where I had fallen, patting the grass and dirt in the hopes of finding the money. The coins were not there. Frantic and worried about returning home without bread or money, I knelt in the grass at the edge of the road, closed my eyes, and asked Heavenly Father to help me find the money so I wouldn't get in trouble. I opened my eyes and immediately in my view was the coin which I proceeded to gather, and I finished my errand as fast as my legs would let me. I was clumsy and young, and had all this change of money, and items to get home. I did not know God but had a sense of knowing He was there when I needed him!

I share this as I have often reflected on the impact of this one event in my life. I had been taught that God existed, taught to pray, and taught God answers prayers; praying at that time was a completely natural response to my problem, and God providing the answer hoped for, was an expected outcome for a young boy like myself!

Knowing who I am and my relationship with God and His son is an unchanging, constant, invariable source of peace and joy. It allows and enables me to see beyond momentary struggles, and have hope of a promised future.

Just as Satan tried to deceive Moses by calling him a "son of man," he wants to deceive each of us from an understanding of who we really are as sons and daughters of God. There is peace and intrinsic joy in truly knowing who we are that frees us from the shackles of Satan's lies.

I hated the controlling desires that so easily had me falling into the Devil's trap. I started rebuking this desire because it was the only way to walk around sin in my life, and grab ahold of true joy and peace.

I encourage you to ponder upon your own life and remember. Too often, through the trials and disappointments in life, we forget what we already know. We forget more than we remember. Instead of doubting our doubts, we forget, and focus only on the present, ignoring both past lessons and future hope. Never forget your past but don't let it affect you. We need to move forward and not let failures affect the joy of what God is landing in our hearts.

In **John 17:3**, He tells us:

> *"And this is eternal life, that they know you, the only true God, and Jesus Christ whom you have sent."*

Knowing and understanding God is no simple task; it is the work of a lifetime. While the study of God is an important part of learning to know Him, I believe the greater part of that learning comes from striving to be like Him. It's a struggle but a fight worth having because the joy of the Lord is amazing. To know God, we must try and be like Him, to be Christ-like in our actions, in our thoughts, in our deeds and our desires; seeing and treating people as he does and doing what He does or would do if he were in our place. We have to be just like Him to walk in joy and let everyone know what time it is!

He is our Creator; He is a teacher, He is a worker, He is married, so yes you should be earnestly striving to get married. He is a Parent, He is a Judge, He forgives, He loves... I could go on listing the attributes of God. All are important, but I would like to focus on a few of the things He does, which I again illustrate with experience.

My mother has been gardening most of her life and encouraged us as children to help her. While still rather young, she encouraged me to work on a small patch of the garden to try and grow my own vegetables. So, I worked, I dug, I weeded, I planted seeds, I watered, and eventually over a period of time, I was able to harvest my first small green cucumber.

To me, it was the sweetest cucumber there ever was, and I remember feeling very proud. It made me happy. I felt joy in the results of my labors.

I share this because we know that God creates. He works. He is the Ultimate Gardener. He is the creator of Heaven and Earth and all things thereon. The work of Creation brings Him joy, and when we emulate that work in the right direction, we feel good. We open ourselves and our souls up to feeling 'joy.'

When we participate or act in doing Godly things, in doing things God does, even in the smallest or simplest of forms, it resonates with who we are.

The Bible is amazingly good to have in your house, ready to pick up, share, and read the chapters.

> *"Wherefore, he that preacheth and he that receiveth, understand one another, and both are edified and rejoice together."*
>
> *- D&C 50:17–22*

Why are we edified? Why do we rejoice? Because we are doing something that is intrinsic to our nature. When we do God-like things, we feel joy. Helping someone or anything that is giving back is a beautiful, blissful feeling. This is what I have learned about my own approach in my experience of being joyful.

God expects each of us to magnify the gifts and talents we have for His purposes. In referring to learning both secular and spiritual things, He educates us on why learning is crucial.

> *"Therefore, verily I say unto you, my friends, call your solemn assembly, as I have commanded you."*
>
> *- D&C 88:121*

Jesus was not demanding or controlling at all. He was passionate and joyful in guiding all of us to the faith.

> *"And He said to them, 'Go into all the world and preach the gospel to all creation.'"*
>
> *- Mark 15:16*

We all have a purpose and mission to fulfill in this life associated with God's plan. The more we prepare ourselves through whatever education we are able to attain, the greater our ability to magnify our talents in God's service and accomplish our mission.

I cannot adequately express how thankful I am for the clear direction I received as a 16-year-old young man staying in school, playing sports, and staying away from the gangs and drugs in the community!

What a blessing to complete my education; it has blessed my life and brought me so much joy. Sometimes we don't hear His voice. We seem to hear other voices and as a young boy I heard God's voice telling me to stay away from what was around me that was bad influence. Even though I was too young to know God or His greatest joy, I did have awareness of His spirit in my life.

I had gotten close to Him once he finally called me to walk in joy and express my own mission to lead and share it.

> *"For behold, this is my work and my glory—to bring to pass the immortality and eternal life of man."*
>
> *- Moses 1:39*

> *"In the sweat of thy face shalt thou eat bread, till thou return unto the ground; for out of it wast thou taken: for dust thou art, and unto dust shalt thou return."*
>
> *- Gen 3:19*

And to Adam, He said,

> *"Because you listened to your wife and ate from the tree about which I commanded you, 'You must not eat of it,' cursed is the ground because of you; through painful toil you will eat of it all the days of your life. It will produce thorns and thistles for you, and you will eat the plants of the field."*
>
> *- Gen 3:17*

There is a satisfaction that comes to those who spend their time and talents on good honest work.

We are not supposed to be idle, the Lamanites are described as **"full of idleness and all manner of abominations"** in **1 Nephi 12:23.**

Ezekiel in describing Sodom's iniquity called it *"an abundance of idleness"* in **Ezekiel 16:49.**

A few years ago, while attending a leadership meeting, I was feeling a little sorry for myself. I had a busy life—young family, and a demanding job in sales, working every weekend and almost never home.

During work one day, around 4PM, one of the sales guys commented on the demands associated with serving in various callings. While I'm sympathetic towards creating getting a balance in life, I believe work is a blessing from God. It is a fundamental principle of salvation, both spiritual and temporal.

If you want to have joy in this life, work, and work hard.

Work on yourself, work on your family, work on your marriage, work on your work and work in favor of God's service. This is a wise choice because nothing can be snatched away from you when it's hard work and God!

As a 16-year-old young man, I started to become more interested in girls. I was in grade 10, which is the equivalent of a sophomore here in the California. I had been pursuing a young lady for several months, and we were "going out" as we called it back then. As somewhat typical teenagers, we were being tempted to participate in inappropriate behavior, and the pressure to do so was building. In an attempt to mitigate the growing temptation, we decided to make a promise to each other—*and God*—that we would not break the commandments.

We wrote it down. In making this promise, I was overwhelmed by a feeling of complete peace, joy, and love as if I was doing the right thing. Being so young and for the first time kissing a girl, or having the thought to go further was scary at the time because it was new, and I felt it was wrong because I had never done it before. I did not fully understand what I had experienced; at the time, I even wondered if this was God telling me that this was the girl I was supposed to marry. We all felt that way, I'm sure, right?

The girl moved away shortly thereafter, and for some reason, there were no more girlfriends for me during my teenage years. Just all those around campus at my high school who did not want to date or I found no connection with. In fact, I blamed the adversary for having no girlfriends for the next three years as I thought Satan had just given up trying to tempt me. What I did learn from that experience is that God is a God of Covenants. This is what a pastor told me one time in a church I attended in Sacramento.

When we approach our covenants with honor and integrity, we will do everything we can to stay true to promises made, and when we do slip up, the power of the redemption of Christ will recognize our honest efforts, and we will have joy in the cleansing power of the atonement. I am speaking of this experience as of 11 years ago from a pastor who kept telling me if we wait, and do right before God, there is no losing in the end.

God keeps His promises and I believe He rejoices when He is able to bless us when we keep our side of the covenants we make. Be true to self, be true to covenants made, be self-respecting, and claim the joy and peace that obedience to covenants enables the faithful to feel. We all have to make that sacrifice to stay close to Jesus in a close covenant connection for pure joy!

Life is not easy. We are each tested and tried, often unfairly, and at times to what we think is our limit. Our hearts break, we struggle, and we feel disappointment and despair. Through these trials, we can learn to appreciate the good in life, and our struggles are often the means of becoming acquainted with God.

Growing up, I always loved being around children. As such, I have always had a desire for a large family. I wanted to have lots of children, five to be exact.

Once I got married, things went differently than I had planned. I found this very hard to understand. Why wasn't God blessing me? Having children is part of His plan. I had one child, a little girl, who is now 12 years old. I thought, '*Why would He deny me this?*'

In my mind, I had been a good, faithful husband and I deserved to be blessed. This is how some of us feel because I also wanted a boy to follow in my steps in playing basketball. After a while, I realized that this was to be my trial. I wouldn't say I liked it. It was hard and challenging to feel the joy I had hoped for in marriage and family. But having a little girl was a blessing, and we can't always get what we want because if it's not God's calling for your life, it's not going to happen!

We would pray and wait on the powers of Heaven, hoping for an answer where none seemed to exist—the absence of this blessing and associated disappointment filtered into other aspects of my life. We sought guidance and strived to carry on.

After the first six years of marriage, the answers finally came, not in my timing or the way I'd initially hoped, but I wouldn't change it for the world. Having a little girl was the best thing that could of happen to us. Through many miracles, we now have one child. Again, we sought the joys and held onto them to sustain us as a happy family. Now that she is 12 years old, I play sports with her, and it's great!

Adam acted in the faith that we all might have joy, each of us must act and exercise faith for ourselves to receive our portion of pleasure in this life.

My daughter is a blessing in my life, and what joy she brings! I cannot help but conclude that without my Eve—my wife—and the leap of faith we took to bind our lives together to God, there would be no lasting or fullness of joy for me.

I testify: God wants us to be happy. He wants us to have joy in this life. As we are obedient, keep our covenants and the commandments, remember who we are, and strive to be like God as we endure the trials of this life, we will and *can* find joy.

CHAPTER 3: KINDNESS

"Be kind and compassionate to one another, forgiving each other, just as in Christ God has forgiven you."

- Ephesians 4:32

The Good Book says we are to be "kind and compassionate with one another." Sometimes that's easier said than done! I used to hate being kind to someone who would not show me kindness. Why should I go out of my way to show kindness to a Person at Work who steps on my feet all the time, cuts me off in conversations, and treats me like a child? Certain things pop up in life that can test your patience and alter your mood, that's for sure. You may have a strained relationship with a family member or a friend, have a conflict at work, or come across something a stranger does that triggers you. (Wouldn't it be nice if everyone drove precisely the way we do—car horns would become a thing of the past!) Needless to say, sometimes we forget that showing kindness takes practice—because we're only human, it doesn't always come naturally. I gathered some Bible verses about kindness to remind us that showing love toward others benefits everybody. It may not seem like it at the moment, but later, it will show that it's all about channeling the love God gives us to those around us.

Don't worry if kindness doesn't come easy to you. God has us covered with Grace to remind you that a bit of time and meditation on kindness can become second nature.

If you're looking for ways to spread kindness and joy to your neighbors, friends, family, co-workers, and even strangers, Love yourself & God first because you have to believe in yourself and have that power; **Acts 1:8** tells us about the Holy Spirit. We must always pick up the cross and Carey's kindness around the neck and show it to the world. Some never expect you when you show kindness or favor. Just do it and be led by the Holy Spirit!

How do we know what kindness looks or behaves like? Christians should always have the wisdom to see the difference between kindness and a good deed, right! We are supposed to be fruit inspectors, and bearing good fruit is having the wisdom to spot it right.

A smile on your way to class, happiness, or a feeling of life is fantastic. Support for a girl with a disability, a free swipe for a commuter, extra tutoring hours offered without extra pay, a door held open for another – we all have experienced acts of kindness. They warm our hearts, bring smiles, and stick with us for years. But is this really what kindness is all about? Should kindness be reserved for one day a year? Is kindness just random acts? Who deserves our kindness? The Bible has much to say about kindness and offers a perfect role model for us to follow – Jesus.

The Christmas season is a time of joy, happiness, and goodwill. Kindness abounds, and a spirit of joviality and love permeates the crisp winter air. The unfortunate reality is that the Christmas spirit of December is quickly followed by the dreary debt of January. Quickly, the season's joy turns into the grind of resolutions, and hearts slowly sink in longing anticipation of spring. The season of kindness is over. But kindness is not a season or a feeling. It should not be reserved for one day out of the year. When these holidays come around, it's like calling families and friends to join for this next year's season holiday to be happy with kindness. There were months and even years passing when my own family members would get together, and once often, we would show kindness out of respect for gathering for the season. Is this genuine kindness or plain respect and showing hospitality?

Instead, kindness is a lifestyle. It is a daily practice. It is a choice. As Christians, we are to grow in the fruit of the spirit – love, joy, peace, patience, goodness, faithfulness, gentleness, self-control, and kindness – and growth takes time and family, right? A seed does not transform into a tree overnight, but with careful watering, tending, and patience, a seed will slowly grow day by day into a solid towering tree. It is the same with kindness. We must be faithful every day to bear the good fruit of kindness. Being kind should be our default mode, a habit of goodwill, a heart of continual service every day of the year. There are so many distractions and letdowns on being kind because we are only human, and feelings never mature or grow up right! When kindness is not perfected or shown in behaviors of the heart, it's not genuine kindness or compassion.

If kindness needs faithful practice every day, kindness also requires intentionality. Now, I'm not saying we should never do random acts of kindness. Often, kind acts are on-the-spot, at the moment, and unplanned. However, we must be intentional. Either plan specific acts of kindness or plan for the random; be ready to do good on the spot. It's not like you have to plan it out or think of it and how to be kind. It's a form of desire and wanting to go out of your way, willing to be you and what's in you for the act of the spirit of kindness that's in you from God. Kindness is not when we feel like it or a random act here or there when we happen to think of it. Kindness requires seeking out, a looking for the needs of others. During his life on earth, Jesus was a perfect emblem of this fruit of the spirit. Jesus showed years of ministry; he looked toward the needs of others, never turning them away. He could be counted on and would not fail you or be mean to you or never not show kindness right! How often today do we miss opportunities to show God's love to others because we are too busy?

We rush here and there, leaving the needs of others in a blur as we walk past the moment of showing kindness. Slow down and open your eyes. Jesus took his time, and you should take your time as well.

So, slow down, make the time, and look for the needs of others. Be intentional in showing kindness; be consistent. I have this issue with moving way too fast and find myself stuck in my own ways rather than God's plan to show kindness and think of others first rather than my own plans or something that's keeping me from putting others first. But why do we have to put strangers first, and they don't put us first? These are questions I always ask myself when sharing the word of God with strangers or even those who struggle with verses in the Bible. I always bring this bible chapter to the topic, knowing it will ease the debate or conversation here to help me explain.

"Love your neighbor as yourself" – the second greatest commandment. But, Lord, "who is my neighbor?" With this question, the Parable of the Good Samaritan was born. A Jewish man was robbed, beaten, and left to die. The Jewish priest and Levite passed by, but the Samaritan saved him. The point of Jesus' story was this: everyone is your neighbor

– the foreigner, the widow, the orphan, and even your enemy. We are to show merciful kindness to everyone. "The Lord watches over the sojourners; he upholds the widow and the fatherless;" "Love your enemies…do good to them that hate you;" "he who does not love his brother, how is it possible for him to love God who is invisible?"

Time and again, God looks out for the cause of the widows and orphans; he cares deeply for the strangers in the land; he emphasizes love for family; he requires mercy and compassion for even your enemies. Often, we want to choose to whom we show kindness. Left to our own, we would limit kind acts to friends and people in authority above us, people from whom we can attain something in return. But Christ calls us to lower our eyes and look at those below, who have nothing, can offer nothing, and have no defender. He calls us to welcome the foreigner, the rejected in our land.

Rather than revenge, He calls us to bless our enemies, knowing that we can soften hearts through kindness. It is easy to get irritated at siblings, throw them under the bus, argue, fight, blame, or just ignore them and not forgive or talk with them again. We have a way of showing ourselves as an enemy at times to those who hurt us or cause harm in our lives that make us feel angry and push us to separate ourselves. I had to learn that Christ emphasizes mercy, patience, love, and kindness to our families. Friends are easy to love, but we are called to be a friend to the friendless. Kindness is selfless, compassionate, and merciful; its most significant power is revealed in practice to our enemies and among the least of these. Love your neighbor; show kindness to *everyone*.

For a perfect emblem of Biblical kindness, we need to look no further than Jesus. Crowds followed Him and traveled miles just to hear him speak. Healing the sick, feeding the hungry, teaching the people, caring for the widow, and defending children, Jesus lived 33 years of perfect kindness. He is not asking any more of us than what He willingly practiced himself. Even on the cross, He displayed compassionate, merciful kindness, praying, "Father, forgive them, for they know not what they do." Defending the weak, poor, and needy, He stated, "As you did it to one of the least of these, my brothers, you did it to me."

Jesus was perfectly selfless in everything He did. I know it's hard to follow or tempting to keep alive in the kindness of behavior. Keep the word close to your heart because it's the road map to kindness. Flowing unceasingly from Him, kindness was His lifestyle. He took notice of the cause of the needy, intentionally and consistently seeking them out, even when He was tired and weary. Without partiality, He was kind to everyone, even if they didn't "deserve" it. He turned no one away. And by shedding his blood on the cross, He demonstrated His love for the entirety of humanity – the ultimate act of kindness. Christ is the perfect role model of kindness.

So, what does Biblical kindness look like? It looks like Christmas, not just us. Not for just a season or one day of the year, kindness is for every moment of every day; it's a habit, a lifestyle, a continual practice. It is intentional, taking time and patience, giving ourselves in "the busy," even when we are "too tired." And kindness is for absolutely everyone. As we intentionally show kindness each day, may we shine the light of Christ to a dying world in need of a savior, a generation in need of love and grace. Be Jesus to someone today and every day; make Him your role model and kindness your lifestyle. Today is a new day of hope, joy, Kindness, and Grace! It's so peaceful to show kindness. It's something the world needs to remember and be different from.

Can you imagine how one must feel after seeing an act of kindness? I fed a homeless shelter one day and had all these water bottles and candy bars passing them out, and once I ran out, there was nothing left to give to those without. It was downtown Sacramento on C street, and I had my daughter with me. We had a little fear, but that fear left once we had the passion for seeing others happy by giving what others needed. It got dark, and doing those hours of passing by alone with my daughter was brave of us because people actually get hurt down there, and danger is always around the corner. We had forgotten all about the time or the place. It became a joy speaking and talking as we spoke on Jesus and giving out everything we had, even my daughter's blanket; we gave to one of the men who needed something warm, and she handed him a blanket along with a $100 bucks of her own savings for an allowance she made helping me over the weeks of cutting and cleaning the lawn back home. It did not matter what we gave or spoke to the men about. It was the time and presence we appeared to them, and at times it's the company of kindness others need, not just giving!

It's incredible what can happen when you are kind and considerate to others. Whether it's a friend, family member, or even a total stranger, simply being kind can open the door for God's favor and kindness to be poured back onto you.

A while back, my brother, Don, was out looking for a new car and thought he had found the one he wanted. The salesman was going to get him some additional information, so Don gave the man his phone number to follow up with him. Several days passed, and Don changed his mind about that particular car. One evening, Don had just come home after a long day at work and sat down to a beautiful bowl of hot noodle soup—his favorite on a cold night. He was just starting to relax when his daughter came over with the phone. "Daddy, Daddy! There's someone on the phone for you."

Reluctantly, Don took the call only to discover it was the salesperson from the car dealership. As soon as he said hello, the salesperson started going on and on about the car Don had looked at more than a week ago. Don was trying to be as lovely as possible and said, "Thank you, but I've decided that car is not big enough, and I have changed my mind." The salesman went on and on about how great the car was as if he didn't even hear what Don had said. Don just sat there staring at that big bowl of noodles—getting cold—trying to be as lovely as possible. "Sir, I've changed my mind about that car," Don said, but the man continued to talk Don into that car. "Would you like to speak with my sales manager?" he asked. Don took a deep breath and had several responses rolling around in his head when suddenly he heard himself say, "Yes." Immediately, he thought, did I just say yes? During the brief moment of silence, he kept reminding himself to be friendly and courteous even though he really wanted to hang up so he could enjoy his dinner!

The manager got on the phone and introduced himself, and said, "I just want to ask you a question—" "Thank you," Don replied, "but really, I've changed my mind about that car." The manager interrupted, "Are you David smiths brother?" he asked. "Yes," Don responded. The manager continued, "I go to Bayside Church, and even if you don't want that particular car, I want to help you find the car you want and get you the very best price possible."

Don hardly knew what to say, but he was grateful he chose to be kind and courteous! Because of his response, God brought him a divine connection. Several weeks later, the sales manager found Don the car he wanted and gave him a price he could hardly believe.

God is no respecter of persons. He'll show you the same favor if you are kind and respectful to people. Whether you are dealing with your spouse, children, grocery clerk, a salesman on the phone, or a homeless person, remember, you are God's representative. Be courteous, gentle, and kind to others, and keep the door open for God to pour out His blessings on your behalf.

I want to talk to you today about being good to people. Everywhere we go, we should look for opportunities to be a blessing. Doesn't have to be something big. You bring your co-worker a cup of coffee in the morning, a small act of kindness. Or on the freeway, traffic backs up. You slow down and let that car in before you, just being good to people. At the grocery store, the person behind you has fewer items. You tell them, "Go up ahead in front of me." Sometimes we just don't care and think of ourselves at the moment. What does it take to get to the level of kindness, or what is that level!

God said to Abraham, "I will bless you, and you will be a blessing." One key to being blessed is, are you willing to be a blessing? God will not increase us in the way he wants if we don't prioritize being good to people.

After the service, I met an older gentleman; he'd been at the pharmacy earlier that week to pick up a prescription. I was getting my medication for my diabetes, and of course, I had my insurance card as they always charge a small $25 fee at the line picking up bottles of medication. One of the other guys waiting in line that stepped up to the counter next to me was fussing and irritated because He thought his insurance would pay more and did not have enough money. I felt his anger and his pain wanting the pills, and he did not have the money to pay. So, I stepped over, knowing he needed help, and out of a kind gesture or whatever you would call it, it was given for his order out of my wallet because who wants to watch someone suffer or be without their medication. Put yourself in that person's shoes or spot in line, empty your wallet or deal with the same issue. A young man in line behind him wanted him to just hurry up and get out of the way because he was in a hurry and seemed to not care about what was going on.

After buying the man's prescription, the older man was so excited he said, "Thanks, sir."

What a blessing because I had no idea how I would pay for this medication I needed. We must see the hood in others, and no matter how hard it seems to show kindness or give, we must practice and learn to be like Jesus!

Galatians 6:10 says, *"As we have therefore opportunity, let us do good unto all men, especially unto them who are of the household of faith."*

If I hadn't been sensitive, not only would he not have been blessed, but when you're good to people, you're sowing a seed for God to be good to you. I would've missed out on a blessing.

You hear your co-worker talking about how they've got to take their car into the shop for repairs."

Hey, can I give you a ride? You need me to swing by and pick you up in the morning"? You're on the lookout. That young couple just had a baby, and you hear them talking about how tired they are, how they're not getting any sleep.

Don't say, "Oh yeah, I remember those days. That's a tough time".

No, be sensitive. That's an opportunity to be a blessing. "Hey, how about my spouse and I come over and babysit? You guys go out to eat one night and have some fun".

Are you looking for ways you can be good to people? The more you bless others, the more God will bless you. I was in a hotel lobby once, and a man was talking on his cell phone when his battery died; it must've been an important call because he was very frustrated and stressed out. He was an Asian man, dressed very nicely, and I was standing next to him, and yes, I heard his conversation and mood swings back and forth. I could not help but make it my own business to step forward and grab my cellphone out and said, "Here, use mine."

He said, "No, I'm calling long distance."

I said, "That's okay; you can call wherever you want to."

He seemed very surprised and said, "Are you sure"? I said, "Yes, I'm sure."

When I heard him calling Korea, I almost changed my mind. Thought, "God, let the call drop, please."

But 5 minutes later, he returned my cell phone and said in the most genuine voice, "Thank you so much."

I could tell that a simple act of kindness had brightened his day. It may have cost me a few dollars, but I've learned when I'm good to other people, God will always be good back to me. Fear always sets in on things like this because we never want to pay the cost for others, and at times it's something we just don't have to reach out to others.

Now, I could've ignored it and thought, "Oh, too bad, his cell phone died, which happens all the time. I don't know the man; it's his problem, not mine". No, I realized my assignment is to be good to people. We know it's a calling to serve Jesus and have that same example he walked in. That's one of the main reasons God has put us here, and if we reach our highest potential, we have to make it a priority to be a blessing. Not just big things, small things. Borrow my cell phone, give a compliment, give a ride home, stay late and help a co-worker. Throughout the day, we should look for ways to be good to people. It does not matter who they are, their origin, their color, or their age! We are saints to show a difference.

A man was standing in line with his small son to buy tickets to the circus. Right in front of him was a young couple with eight small children. They were all under the age of 12. They were well-behaved and clean-cut, but he could tell by what they were wearing they didn't have a lot of money, and they were so excited about going to the circus; the young couple stepped up to the counter. The man asked proudly for eight children's tickets and two adults.

His wife dropped her head when the attendant told them how much it would cost. The husband leaned closer and said, "How much did you say it would be"? The attendant told them again, and he didn't know what to say. It was apparent he didn't have enough money. The man in line behind him, watching all this take place, pulled $40 out of his pocket and discretely dropped it on the ground.

He picked it up and said, "Excuse me, sir, I think this money may have fallen out of your pocket." The man looked at him, knowing exactly what he was doing. He said with a small tear running down his cheek, "Thank you, sir, from the bottom of my heart." How kind and good and loving can you be right! Everyone does not have this kind of thought process or kindness to just give or create a difference in one's life struggle or something similar. We don't like to go out of our way nowadays for strangers. The Bible tells us to entertain strangers so that we might be entertaining angels.

You don't have to. There's nothing wrong if you don't, but you're on the lookout for ways that you can be good to be people. On the forefront of your mind is not, "How can I get blessed"? But, "How can I be a blessing"?

I've learned if you will make somebody else's day, God will always make your own day. If you bring a smile to their face, God will bring it to your face, and this is the most rewarding way to live; not, "What can I get"? But, "What can I give"? Not, "What can you do for me"? But, "What can I do for you"?

The scripture says, "Jesus went about doing good, healing all that were sick." The first thing Jesus did before healing, before ministering, and before delivering was he was good to people, and we all have an assignment. You could say we all have a ministry. May not be up in front of people, may not go overseas and be a missionary. Our ministry is to be good to people. That's one of the best witnesses that we could ever have. Confess that Christ is number one in your life and that others are before you. Jesus had this attitude all the time. Yes, trying to be this person or walk in the shoes of Jesus' sandals is a challenge. You must be called and born again to see Jesus's lifestyle change. We don't have to do things to feel we are saved or getting points or blessings ahead of us. I used to think like this and thought it was just being good and kind, but there is more than just those actions.

You don't necessarily have to preach them a sermon. You don't have to argue doctrine; try to make them believe what you believe. Just be good to them. Our actions speak much louder than our words. We can say all day long, "I love you," but true love is seen in what we do. If I really love you, I'll be good to you. If I love you, I'll let you have the parking spot even though I got there first. I'll prefer you.

God said to Abraham, "I will bless you, and you will be a blessing." One key to being blessed is, are you willing to be a blessing? God will not increase us in the way he wants if we don't prioritize being good to people.

After the service, I met an older gentleman; he'd been at the pharmacy earlier that week to pick up a prescription. He thought his insurance would pay more for it, and he did not have enough money. There was a young man in line behind him that attended Church. He'd just finished working out and ran to get something to drink. He overheard this conversation about how the man didn't have enough money. He said to him, "You stay here. I'll be back in 10 minutes".

He ran home, got his wallet, returned, and bought the man's prescription. The older man was so excited he said, "Ralph, I came to Church today for the first time because if there are people like that at Church, then I want to be here."

Friends, being good to people is better than preaching a sermon. Being kind, generous, and compassionate speaks much louder than words, and we should have a daily goal to do at least one good thing for somebody else. Don't wait for a special occasion. Doesn't have to be Christmas, their birthday, their anniversary, or Valentine's. No, just an ordinary day, bring your spouse home some flowers. Show her you care, and the fighting is the enemy upset with us because we love each other and won't give in to the devil's tricks. Reach over and tell her you to love her more and more!

You're at the mall, and you see that blouse that would look good on your friend, buy it and take it to her. "What's this for? It's not my birthday. It's not Christmas". "No, it's because you're my friend, and I want to be good to you." You don't even know that young man who delivers pizza to your house. But sometimes, for no reason at all, bless him with an extra $20.

You can't be good to everyone, but you can be good to the people God put in your path. You need to study them. Listen to what they're saying, be sensitive to their needs. A man was helping me on a project, and he said in passing, "Wow, Ralph, your computer monitor is so clear. The clarity and the sharpness are amazing". I said, "Yes, it is, and what kind of monitor do you have"? He said, "Oh man, my monitor's like eight years old. It's not clear". The following week, he had a monitor just like mine.

Here's my point: when you're kind to people in their time of need, God will make sure somebody will be kind to you. Your gifts will come back to you. Every opportunity you have, be good to people. You don't know why God has put that person in your path. It's not a coincidence. God has strategically lined up every person, every detail, and every step of your life. He is in control, for sure! How do we continue being happy doing what we are called to do?

Everybody wants to be happy. But how can we meet that sometimes elusive goal? This was a difficult question even before the global pandemic, but nowadays, just thinking about it can seem futile. Parents are trying to balance their new lives online now as school teachers. People who live alone try to keep their focus in isolation. When life is measured by back-to-back Zoom meetings, even taking a shower can seem like a win.

The transformation of the workplace into scheduled online meetings has led to another source of deprivation: The removal of hard work. For many people, hearing a colleague say, "Thank you so much" in the hallway or a manager telling you, "Great job" after a presentation was a highlight of office life. Now, these seem like traditions from another lifetime. Without water cooler interactions, casual lunches, and coffee breaks with colleagues, we don't have the same opportunities for social connection. Without them, finding joy in our work can be much more complicated. So, what can we do about it?

We offer a humble suggestion: Kindness. This past year, most management advice has focused on sustaining productivity during the pandemic, yet the power of kindness has been largely overlooked. Practicing kindness by giving compliments and recognition can transform our remote workplace.

The Benefits of Kindness

A commitment to be kind can bring many significant benefits. First, and perhaps most obviously, practicing kindness will benefit our colleagues. Being recognized at work helps reduce employee burnout and absenteeism, and improves employee well-being; receiving a compliment, words of recognition, and praise can help individuals feel more fulfilled, boost their self-esteem, improve their self-evaluations, and trigger positive emotions, and they will. These positive downstream consequences of compliments make intuitive sense: Praise aligns with our naturally positive view of ourselves, confirming our self-worth.

Second, practicing kindness helps life feel more meaningful. For example, spending money on others and volunteering our time improves well-being, bringing happiness and a sense of meaning to life. Being kind brings a sense of meaning because it involves investing in something bigger than ourselves. It shapes how others perceive us, improving our reputation and view of ourselves. We and our acts of kindness make us believe that we have what it takes to be a good person. It's something important we all need to cultivate into many lives and our own.

CHAPTER 4: GOODNESS

"Oh, taste and see that the LORD is good! Blessed is the man who takes refuge in him!"

- Psalms 34:8

What does it mean to taste and see that the Lord is good? When I first found or stumbled across that verse, reading it, sitting there all alone thinking what it was telling me was all put together in everything I had started reading. It seems odd to "taste" the Lord, doesn't it? And if we're Christian, a man or woman of faith, don't we already know the Lord is good? Maybe. Maybe not!

Where this scripture is found, it tells a story of murderous threats, insanity, and praise for God. I thought, how can I praise God? At the same time, it's dangerous. Interesting mix, isn't it? But more likely, this verse—not to mention our walk with Christ—has a more profound impact than what we see at the surface level. Maybe we're meant to go deeper. Maybe God has used you and me to see, depose and express the feeling of taste or something more substantial.

Goodness Defined

We sing about it, and we say it often. But do we fully understand this attribute of God? Meditate on the goodness of God with me this morning. The Bible defines God's goodness in two ways. One has to do with His character; the other focuses on His actions. **Ps. 119:68** captures both when it says of God: *"You are good, and what you do is good; teach me your decrees."*

The first half of that verse focuses on the fact that God is by nature good. He is "morally excellent, extraordinarily beautiful, deeply glad, and extravagantly bountiful." But since this is God we're talking about, this goodness ascribed to Him is raised to the highest possible levels.

Think about it: God is the original definition of good. He is good in and of Himself. For us, goodness is an added quality. But it comes naturally for Him. God is not just the greatest of beings; He is the Best. We think we are the best or made to be the best! We are fragile and broken and, most of all, unsaved in a world of chaos and blinded. Jesus never was blinded or lost or full of hate. We are made and put here for a purpose. What do you think that purpose is? How do we define ourselves in a fallen world of hate and rejection? Look around you and see all the pain, suffering, and hate.

That's precisely what Jesus meant when He said, "*No one is good except God alone.*" (**Mark 10:18**).

We call all kinds of things good - "This steak is good. He's a good friend. That was a good movie." But all we call "good" on this earth is tainted and imperfect. God alone is goodness itself. There is nothing good in us because we are full of sin and born into sin. So, what's the new nature we should walk in? What does it take to be free of this terrible bondage of what the Bible calls slaves of sin!

But how do you see the true character of a person? By his actions. The fruits of the spirit are a sign of actions (A lousy tree vs. good tree.) So the second strand of definition for God's goodness concentrates on what He does. And the Bible is replete with descriptions that point to His kindness, mercy, steadfast love, and generosity. God is disposed to give to human beings beyond all deserving, all the time.

Have you ever thought of God as generous toward you? Can you believe that when He looks at you with all your baggage, junk, and hang-ups, He says, "I want to be generous to you? I can't wait to pour out that which will make you happy - not because you deserve it, but because there's something about Who I am that loves to overflow in extravagant ways upon you."

The Bible says those are actually God's thoughts about you. God is for you. I used to think he was against me because I did not play in the NBA or was raised in a happy home with both parents that could give my siblings and me what it takes to have a successful future. I know now that God has my back. He has your back as well! He is there, plotting to do you good. You are the object of His affection, and because of His divine nature, all He expresses comes from an expansive, overwhelming, God-sized generosity toward you.

But maybe you just can't go there this morning. Maybe your circumstances are so mundane, your life so hard, and your options so few that saying "God is good" feels hollow. Let me help you see through the lenses the Bible supplies.

Clean Blessings

This is the lowest level at which He expresses His goodness and the one we tend to overlook or take for granted. But David saw it clearly. God moved him to write Ps. 145 - a hymn of praise that celebrates God's goodness expressed in the created order.

In **v. 3-4**, he shouts out, *"Yahweh is great and is highly praised; His greatness is unsearchable. One generation will declare Your works to the next and proclaim Your mighty acts."* And **v. 7-9** describes what the older generation will say to the younger: *"They will give a testimony of Your great goodness and will joyfully sing of Your righteousness. The Lord is gracious and compassionate, slow to anger, and great in faithful love."* Notice **v. 9**: *"The Lord is good to everyone..."*

Who is included in the word "everyone"? You are. If we missed that, he repeats the idea in the following phrase: "His compassion [rests] on all He has made." That means you can go nowhere in the universe where God won't be good to you. He is everyplace and won't leave or not show up. You see, we think he does not show up or answer our prayers or needs when we have asked, and nothing seems to change for the better in what we ask. He here the cry of the voice and heart at all times.

All eyes look to You, and You give them their food in due time. You open Your hand and satisfy the desire of every living thing. The Lord is righteous in all His ways and gracious in all His acts." Every relationship, every job, every tree, every taste of food that pleases us, every birdsong, every friend, and flower and field are a reminder of His compassion for us. Look in every corner of this world and every part of your day, and you will find the overflow of His generosity if you only begin to look for it.

Psalm 107 is devoted to this theme and opens with joy: *"Give thanks to the Lord, for He is good; His faithful love endures forever. Let the redeemed of the Lord proclaim that He has redeemed them from the hand of the foe..."* Then the psalmist describes four different scenarios where God graciously steps in to reveal His goodness. I don't have time to unfold each one; just touch on it:

God comes to the rescue of people frantically searching for something or someone that will satisfy their souls. When they cry out to the Lord, He will deliver them, and their soul will find their true home. I had cried out to God many times in solitary and saw his love reach out to my hands and touch me with his presence. He is so worthy of being praised and respected!

God intervenes in the lives of those who rebelled against God's Word and suffer for it. When they repent, He delivers them from their distress, breaks the chains of sin that bind them, and turns the night to day. If he did it for me in that suffering time of my life, he would do the same for you! Give God a chance to take over your life and lead you in the right direction.

God intervenes on behalf of His goodness in the lives of foolish people who had given themselves to sin and find its death-bringing results touching their relationships and lives. When they cry to the Lord. He heals them and reverses the deadly effects of sin in their lives. It is a beautiful feeling to know the Lord is behind the whole thing. I was so chosen to see how he has worked in my life today. Here I am explaining the details of the Bible I have learned and breaking it down into parts that can teach one the basics of how Jesus works.

God rescues those pounded by calamity. When the storms threaten to sink us, and we're at our wit's end, we can call to Him and see Him command the storms to be still because He is good.

He's been there for you more than you'll ever know. Regardless of your situation this morning, God is the best person to take it to. There is no surer source of deliverance or blessing than Him because He is always good. He has treated me and my mistakes with forgiveness.

Respond to his spirit!

The goodness of God calls for a response. Let me give you three specific steps we must take to change our lives and begin to fully experience the effects of God's generosity.

1. Repent of unbelief and ingratitude

Romans 2:4 says, "*Or do you presume on the riches of his kindness and forbearance and patience, not knowing that God's kindness is meant to lead you to repentance?*"

Paul says, "*Do you think all these blessings that visit your days came because you're just an incredibly nice person who made God's special list? No, His goodness was meant to lead you to Him.*"

Going through your life receiving what He has been giving without trusting in Christ is like saying, "God, I had all this coming. I deserve this and more. So keep it coming." We want the gifts, not the Giver. Our ingratitude and greed for what He can do for us while rejecting Him are the heights of sin. And one day, the gravy train will come to an end.

Stop. Look around you. See the hand of the Lord in your life and turn to Him today. Put an end to taking from God and learn to thank Him.

2. Rest in His goodness when adversity comes

We live in a world where bad things happen to good people, and good things happen to bad people. Sometimes, our circumstances argue with us about how good God is. Sometimes God's good plan for us means going through trials, losses, heartache, and death.

But hear me: He is there for you. **Ps. 31:19-20** says:

*"How abundant are the good things
that you have stored up for those who fear you,
that you bestow in the sight of all,
on those who take refuge in you.
20 In the shelter of your presence you hide them
from all human intrigues;*

you keep them safe in your dwelling
from accusing tongues."

God has perfect goodness stored up for you. Take your refuge in Him. Rest there for a season. He is up to more than you know and has hidden help that only comes when you give it to Him.

3. Step out in faith. Don't waver.

When you believe that God is good all the time, it frees you to take ever-increasing steps of faith. In our kitchen, we have a beautiful sign print of Jeremiah 29:11 that reminds me of God's intent toward my family and me: "For I know the plans I have for you" the Lord's declaration - "plans for your welfare, not for disaster, to give you a future and a hope." Believing that removes you from fear of taking risks for Christ's sake. **Psalm 84:11** is fuel to the fire of daring greatly for Him: "*For the Lord God is a sun*" (He illuminates the path we should all take) "and shield" (He protects us) "(the Lord gives Grace and glory (that's exaltation for those who follow Him). "He does not withhold the good from those who live with integrity." You never miss out if you step out with God.

Had anyone ever given to you suspected nothing in return? There are very good giving people who will bless you according to God's will and path for your life.

Have you ever been given a gift you could have never gotten for yourself? Has anyone ever sacrificed a considerable amount for you without getting anything in return? Think about your past and your thoughts on giving or blessing someone.

Has anyone ever said that you were a good person? Is being good something you strive to be or aspire toward?

We must learn about bringing our best to everything we do daily. She begins by exploring the meaning of goodness:

Is goodness the same as happiness? We desire appetitively because of our bodies. We desire emotionally because of our sense of self in contact with other human beings. And we also have rational desires to understand how to do what's best. Our goodness requires all these capacities to be developed and expressed.

This can be a lifelong process that is never perfectly realized but should always be struggled for. "Goodness is impermanent and organic, meaning it can progress as well as regress," that is why we must be steadfast in caring for ourselves and the world at large. "In politics and culture, in the media and corporations, we have cultivated conditions that have produced a lot of violence, discrimination, and despair for which there is a collective level of responsibility."

Because many of us have a complicated relationship with what it means to be good, it can help to reframe the subject and widen it. "Some people flinch when they ponder whether or not they or others are 'good' because the words 'good' and 'goodness' have long been associated with obedience," As an author and Christian."

"I reject that definition! Goodness is expressed through loving, kindness, generosity of spirit and deed, and thoughtful consideration of others. It can be as simple as offering to let someone ahead of you in line and as complicated as making years-long sacrifices for your freedom because someone you love needs your help. Throughout a lifetime, most of us do both." My suggestion is to be kind!

"Kindness is at the center of what it means to be good. It may require very little from us or the opposite. It may require words and action or restraint and silence. Everything can be said with kindness. I know that's tuff to do when someone offends you or attacks you or even a person Cyberbullying you every time you open the Google search and see your name as if they made it a monster. Every tough position we have to take can be taken with kindness. How do we do this and stay on the rim of being kind? What does it take in a time of hardship with No exceptions but to stay kind? Being a good person requires working toward that unrealized world where the dignity and integrity of all human beings, all life, are honored and respected." It's been a long road for me and growing struggles because I felt I needed a time out and away from the constant test I was faced with giving up. I had to be alone, find goodness within myself, and face reality's doors that I have opened for my own choices that brought me to where I am today.

Some of those doors were darkened with tears and tragically tore my heart into crying out to God. I had to see a door that was a breakthrough with some light coming from it. It's been long suffering from the doors I had chosen, that's for sure.

To stop and come back to the present moment and enjoy our breathing is what I was craving instead of the past. We stop to recognize what is happening within us and around us: our feelings, our thinking, whether our body is relaxed or in tension, who is in front of us, or what we are doing. With repetition, we begin to see and understand ourselves better — and choose to do one thing rather than another."

I ask myself hard questions.

"As a public speaker life coach, I tend to look at what has lifted us when we found ourselves at our lowest — what has called us to a better place. How are we, as a nation and as a people, using life itself to create good for the poor and broken and captive and for those who are made to feel unaccepted? I desire the best, as we call goodness for all kinds, period! We must constantly raise that question as we live — seeking to answer it individually and together. We need to embrace those deepest moral values that call us to, first and foremost, seek love, truth, justice, and concern for others."

Hold yourself accountable and that you have goodness in your actions.

"You have to know your different motivations, how strong they are, and if you can get some of them to pull against the others. I was a lost soul in my 20s and 30s. Like many of us, right! , I resolved to quit on multiple occasions from sinning and living a life of chaotic choices. I knew if I ever walked in sin, living and breathing those choices again, I would have to face the consequences!

The Bible instructs us to Go and sin no more unless something worse happens to us. Let's face it, I have no choice but to be good, kind, gentle, and pure in spirit because it's a better life here on earth! The goodness of God leads us to repentance and a new start.

CHAPTER 5: PEACE

"Peace I leave with you, my peace I give unto you: not as the world giveth, give I unto you. Let not your heart be troubled, neither let it be afraid."

- John: 14:27

No matter who we are or how life is currently going, one inevitable thing is that our faith will be tested. We will feel incomplete and as if we never have peace!

These challenges can range from our everyday struggles and disappointments to life-changing losses. The movement of our faith in God, our faith in relationships, and our faith in life – is revealed during these testing times. Now days have been challenging to understand faith in a world of hate, jealousy, unloving, racism, doubts, and, most of all, nonbelievers!

"Count it all joy, my brothers, when you meet trials of various kinds, for you know that the testing of your faith produces steadfastness. And let steadfastness have its full effect, that you may be perfect and complete, lacking in nothing."

- James 1:2-4

Tests, pressure, setbacks, failure, and trouble force our faith into the open and reveal its true colors. We need Bible verses about resilience like this to help us believe those challenges don't have to own us. We can take control and rule the direction God wants us in!

In football, the term "front runner" describes an enthusiastic, energetic, and engaged player while the game goes their way and the team is winning. But as soon as they encounter a setback or fall behind in the game, they collapse – quickly retreating, they make less effort and eventually give up. Have you ever felt this type of setback or challenge? Of course, you have other storms in your life, right?

Lately, I have started to see myself as a "spiritual front-runner." Friends have been helping me see my weaknesses and sins as they pertain to my faith, marriage, relationships, and leadership, and I have not responded well. Typically, I am enthusiastic, but facing these truths has made me angry and self-piteous. I seem to keep failing and falling as if I never had what it takes to stay on the battlefield and fight! We must keep pushing and knowing that it's always a rewarding feeling after reaching the level of getting through the test and reaching a sense of peace.

It's a far cry from the "sheer gift" attitude described in James 1. That is one of my favorite chapters because it explains the truth about self and peace! We ask with the wrong motives and never get what we want because the motives expect something in return when it is not there to achieve or grab hold of.

God is helping me to become mature, well-developed, and ready for the next stage of my life. At least I noticed I needed him to show me the way!

I am learning that God is using these challenges to help me understand the reality of the condition of my faith.

By forcing me to confront the truth, God is helping me to become mature, well-developed, and ready for the next stage of my life.

What obstacles are you facing in your life that God is using to mature, develop and prepare you for the next step of your future? There is always something to learn and know about yourself that will show you need more development in your walk with God and peace.

From birth to death, there are four life-defining stages. We all grow, develop and mature as we continue to move on. For some, transitioning from one stage to another feels like a natural process, while others find themselves stuck in a stage for decades. Sadly, some might even skip a stage without learning the essential lessons of a given stage!

We go through a few distinct stages of life once we are ready. These stages are true for all humans throughout their life. Closely watching the life of our mentors, family, and friends allows one to recognize patterns behind these different phases of life. This can help you shift gears regarding your growth and pursuit of success and peace.

Stage 1: Imitation and Education

The first stage represents all the basics of life. You learn how to walk, talk and do simple tasks like feeding yourself. In this stage, life is focused on education and building the foundation for your life. How? Simply imitating what you see others do. Who? All those adults around you, your teachers, parents, and even superheroes, they'll show you how to function.

As a baby, you are helpless and dependent upon others for survival. You eat, sleep and breathe. Your mind is at peace while the brain develops, picking up sensory abilities and motor skills. Thinking of how I developed, looking back and moving forward, I had to see a lot growing up fast and skipping areas that others may not have.

By later childhood, you move on to more challenging tasks while still depending on adults to guide you. By imitating others, you gradually develop social and similar skills and learn to fit in with society.

You start to observe the rules and norms that surround you. You want to be accepted by society, and your friends on the bloke and the kids at school are growing. Therefore, you obey these rules and adapt to these norms. It's like following the crowd and doing as others do around you.

The fundamental objective of all of this is to help us become self-regulated adults. Please remember that you still depend upon others for guidance and seek their approval. Out of all the stages of life, this one helps us to lie the proper foundation.

You remain in the first stage from birth until late adolescence or early adulthood. The greatest danger you can encounter during this stage is not letting go of the need for external validation. I had a severe struggle with letting go and feeling left out when I was not validated or accepted.

You might get trapped by adults that do not approve of you becoming independent. Some adults are not suited for teaching. They come up with forms of punishment that can prevent us from developing true independence. We can easily be misleading to others and think we know it all at times.

The next stage is when you dare to place your values above the validation of others and start acting for yourself.

"It's not hard to make decisions once you know your values."

As the first stage taught you to fit in, the second will teach you to stand apart. You are ready to discover who you are in this time of life. You are now making your own decisions and learning what makes you unique from others. We all have different options in life and qualities about ourselves that would lead others astray to peace or bring them to knowing true peace and purpose.

The end of adolescence marks the beginning of your journey into adulthood, which is the most prolonged phase of the human life cycle. You completed your education, and your focus lies now on acquiring an excellent job. It's the time when you start to explore life and go out to leave your mark on the world.

In addition, you develop a strong desire to explore life, increasing your willingness to take risks.

You start to experiment with new and exciting possibilities. You will make many, and I mean many, mistakes, learning from trial and error. I have made so many mistakes and learned the hard way, that's for sure! You will live in many places, try different food, and experiment with various activities. You might also have numerous relationships with lovers and friends in this stage, like being married and divorced or heartbroken from long relationships and feeling destroyed or taken advantage of from a partnership.

The second stage can be highly pleasurable and exciting. Therefore, some people do not wish ever to leave this stage. Instead of allowing their development to unfold, they prefer to continue life on this level. Also, you will notice your limitations at some point, which will anger you. You probably start by not accepting these limitations and pushing to achieve them regardless.

With time, you learn that your limitations are real and that they are a good thing. They show you what you're bad at; you can't be great at everything. The second stage is accomplished once we realize we must be selective about our actions. Limitations will help you transition into stage three.

"If you accept your limitations, you go beyond them."

Stage 2: Dedication and Commitment

So, you have allowed your developments to unfold and accepted your limitations. In this stage, you begin to arrange your priorities as you see fit. You evaluate what you are good at and what benefits your life — also called being selective. You don't want to bring needless luggage from stage One with you. This could be harmful activities or places.

After you have cut away the unimportant aspects, you start to get serious about what you have kept. For example, your focus is now on your career and the development of a young family. Stage three marks a significant number of responsibilities, not only for ourselves but also for others. At this point, you start to build your legacy.

Building your legacy is about leaving something behind when you are gone. You begin the foundation for this legacy at stage three, including priorities and responsibilities. Most people in stage three want to leave the world a better place than how they found it.

For some, the ambition to accomplish even more never ends. People are so used to constantly striving for more that they have anxiety about retirement. And once that day comes, the hunger for accomplishments and power starts to haunt them, and they miss out on the following essential stage in life.

Someplace down the line, we missed the area of peace! Jesus is known as the Prince of Peace.

King is the one who makes it to the top with his dedication, but the prince was born with liability.

A son or daughter of a king directly becomes the prince or princess, but the real person who makes them the prince and princess is the king, like how Jesus was called the prince of peace because his parents were the true king and queen of peace.

Jesus was given to us and called the Prince of Peace, and we called him the wonderful counselor, the mighty God who listens to all of our problems and provides us the solution to them.

But the Biblical Peace Story states that Jesus is the prince of peace because of the king and the queen.

The same is in our lives; if your parents are peaceful, lovely, and loving, we will become the same. We are nothing but the shadows of our parents. I was the shadow of my mother, who raised six boys and one older girl, and we all had her example of love and treating others with kindness.

3. Wicked people will not know peace

The Lord says that if a person is evil or intends to be morally wrong, he will never be able to achieve peace in his life.

Unless you stop throwing that hate and anger toward other people and your inner self, you will never be able to kill that evil inside you, which will always be a brick between you and the peace.

Another point mentioned in this peace story in the Bible is your wrong intentions, and the intentions come from within. Always keeping your intentions morally correct will lead to a state where you can achieve peace, as the Lord said.

Moral correctness comes from positivity and happiness, which makes your inner self happier.

4. We can have peace with God

The Lord stated that we could have peace with God. A priest is closest to God, and you will never see anyone being more peaceful than a priest because he is the closest to God.

This peace story in the Bible mentioned that the Lord was torn apart internally and molested against the law of conduct because of his iniquities, and on top of it was the chastisement that brought us peace.

The Lord was wounded, and his wounds were the ones that made us all heal. If you want peace, you should get under the shadows of God when you see the chastisement occurring on him and surely bring peace for you.

5. *"Therefore if thou bring thy gift to the altar, and there rememberest that thy brother hath ought against thee."* - **Matthew's 5:23**

This peace story in the Bible states that if you present a sacrifice at the altar in the temple but also if you know that there is a person who has a grudge or hates you, then you should not make that sacrifice; you should leave that sacrifice at the altar, firstly you should go and reconcile to that person.

If you are sure that he does not carry any grudge or hate towards you, you can return to the temple at the altar and offer your sacrifice to God.

Also, another peace story in the Bible about "Make peace with others quickly" states that if you are going to court with your lawyer, if you and your lawyer had any previous differences in the past, it can harm your case.

You should first sort those differences with your lawyer as quickly as possible because once you are in court and if your lawyer loses the case against the accuser by the judges' judgment, they will hand you over.

The officer and the officer will throw you inside a prison, and you will not be accessible again unless you pay every penny the judge has fined you.

"Let not your hearts be troubled, neither let them be afraid."

- John 14:27

The peace which is given by the world is different from the peace we've all got from the almighty God!

This world has given us peace of satisfaction, peace of pleasure by the intake of intoxicants or excessive eating of food, but in this peace story in the Bible is mentioned that the peace we get from God is different from the peace we get in everyday life.

This peace is a gift of God; it is peace of mind and heart that this world can never give us. The peace story also states that this gift that God has given us will keep us away from troubles in our life and make us fearless.

We should not be afraid as we all have peace of mind and heart as a gift of God in our lives.

CHAPTER 6: PATIENCE

"**P**atience is a virtue." We're all familiar with that cliché, and many of us know Paul lists that patience in **Galatians 5:22-23** as among the fruit of the Spirit.

So there's no disputing that the Christian ought to be patient. But as with most virtues, biblical writers assume that we know what patience is and don't give an explicit definition. But do we? Yes, this is a struggle of mine. I have dealt with this topic all my life and lived the Christian lifestyle.

Could you define patience if you were asked? And, to make things trickier, could you do so without citing examples of patience? Starting with the basic definition of patience as "waiting without complaint," Why is patience a virtue? What are the different varieties of patience? Why is patience so tricky at times? And how is patience developed? Ask yourself this question: Do you always walk and think with patience?

I see patience as a virtue.

When defined as "waiting without complaint," patience might seem to be a morally insignificant trait. What's so virtuous about not complaining? In itself, not complaining carries no particular virtue. Suppose I'm waiting for the arrival of a friend from out of town, and she spends the time happily reading or watching television. We wouldn't say that simply because she's not complaining; she exhibits patience in this case. Something else must be required to make one's lack of complaint virtuous. That something is discomfort. Because a circumstance is uncomfortable for someone, we find her refusal to complain remarkably and thus regard her as a patient.

So to improve the initial definition above, to be patient is to endure discomfort without complaint. This calls into play some other virtues, specifically, self-control, humility, and generosity. That is, patience is not a fundamental virtue but a complex of other virtues.

An example from the life of Christ illustrates this. Jesus was very patient with his disciples. He was even more patient with us; all are nasty ways to change and come to him for salvation. His followers were sometimes thickheaded, lazy, selfish, and slow to believe. Even from a mere human standpoint, we can see how frustrating they must have been. How much more irritating it would be for God Incarnate to interact daily with these men. Despite Jesus' miracles and words of wisdom, they were focused on themselves and wavered in their belief about who he was.

We do the same thing and have fallen short of God's glory daily, haven't we? I have turned my back on God and screwed things up for those around me and, most of all, myself. To say that was uncomfortable for Jesus would be an understatement. Yet do we find him railing at his disciples over their foolishness and stupidity? Or making fun of them when they make mistakes? Jesus does point out the sin in us for sure.

Occasionally, he remarks that his disciples are slow to believe, or he asks rhetorically how long they will fail to have faith in him. Still, these are always appropriate reminders about what was at stake for them. These were fitting and useful rebukes, not petty venting. He cared for them, and we should respect that God risked his all for us on the cross. I know it's a complex concept to picture as having unbelievers accept this truth. I used to mock the word that approached me through someone else while God, on the other end, was trying to get my attention before it was too late.

Notice that Jesus' refusal to complain about his irritating disciples can be described as an exercise of self-control. Indeed he would have been justified in blistering them with insults. It's worth noting that his omniscience guaranteed every possible joke and the embarrassing remark was at his disposal on any particular occasion. This makes his self-control even more admirable.

His refusal to complain also involves humility, the conscious decision to lower himself by not exercising his right, as the holy man he was, to judge and dismiss his friends because of their faults. We might even say this is a form of mercy.

Finally, Jesus' refusal to complain about his disciples is generous. Despite their vice and thick-headedness, he remained no less committed to them and served them increasingly as their failures became more outstanding.

While the patience of Christ is exceptional in many respects, the basic features of this virtue are indeed the same wherever it appears. Patience involves such things as self-control, humility, and generosity, all of which are themselves virtues. So one might say that patience is a virtue because it exercises several other virtues.

Distinguishers of Patience

What are the different contexts in which patience is demonstrated? One way to distinguish types of patience is based on the nature of the discomfort involved. The following threefold distinction can be made.

The first type is the patience needed when facing a nuisance. A person or a set of circumstances irritates you, and you'd love to complain, but you hold your tongue, knowing that such a grievance would be petty or compound the problem. That is hard to hold anger and patience back to control the temptation that easily tempts us to give in to that person at the office who is so insufferably annoying and doesn't, after all, mean to bug you. And what good will it do to moan about those potholes on your street? So you quietly endure these things. Did you know you were being virtuous in doing so?

A second type of patience is called for when facing boredom. Those who fall into a rut at work or home often experience discomfort over the uneventful routine. To those who don't struggle with boredom, it might seem absurd to suggest it can be a severe trial. But those who endure the plague of drab routine without complaint exhibit the virtue of patience.

A third type of patience is the most serious and significant. It is the patience required when one suffers in some way, either physically or psychologically. Patience is required if you're struggling with some disease or mental illness. Or if you must assist someone else who suffers, a family member or friend, you are called upon to be patient.

Whether you bear the burden of affliction directly or indirectly, your challenge is to endure that discomfort. This doesn't mean you shouldn't cry out in your distress. Scripture advises us to do just that, so it's appropriate because the degree of discomfort in some situations warrants complaint. But this raises some important questions: What is a complaint? And which complaints are worthy of it?

Is It Ever Okay to Complain?

To complain is to make known one's irritation or frustration about some matter. This doesn't necessarily imply that we should say anything out loud. Usually, we complain by speaking directly about the circumstance that bothers us. But we also complain in nonverbal ways, with a sigh, a huff, a shake of the head, or a roll of the eyes. Many of us are pretty expert at communicating our irritation in subtle ways to those closest to us through means that most people wouldn't recognize as complaining. But our target complainee (the person we complain to) gets the message, and that's all that matters.

Which complaints, then, are worthy? Indeed, it's legitimate to raise objections about unjust or impractical conditions that need to be changed. But grumbling over things that are merely annoying or against one's wishes is petty. And complaining about things that cannot be changed doesn't qualify as a legitimate protest. So a worthy complaint is neither petty nor pointless.

Complaint to God is inappropriate only when its cause is insignificant. Major physical and psychological afflictions are significant, so patiently enduring them may involve complaint.

Thus, complaining to God in prayer is not vicious but virtuous. It is a valid complaint to someone sovereign and therefore in control of whatever concerns us. In the Bible, I remember reading the book of Psalms, which showed me how complaints arise and let me see differently. Examples of godly complaints, such as the following:

From my youth, I have been afflicted and close to death;

"I have been sick and close to death since my youth. I stand helpless and desperate before your terrors. Your fierce anger has overwhelmed me. Your terrors have paralyzed me. They swirl around me like floodwaters all day long. They have engulfed me completely. You have taken away my companions and loved ones. Darkness is my closest friend."

- Psalm 88:15

This is, indeed, a complaint, but the severity of the suffering calls for it. Most importantly, God is the recipient of the complaint. So this is an act of faith on the psalmist's part, affirming divine sovereignty even over his terrible pain. Can you imagine the pain and suffering of this? It's like, why do we have to deal with so much of this? I have to say that God is patient with us through it all.

Patience with People and God

This point suggests yet another way to categorize patience, one premised upon the biblical idea that God continually sustains the whole universe. God governs every occurrence in nature, so even "natural" events, as it turns out, have a personal explanation—namely, God himself. This means that all patience or impatience is ultimately patience or impatience with someone. This did not make sense to me until I had to read it over many times again and again.

Therefore, two categories of patience can be distinguished based on the person (or persons) with whom we must be patient. We know it's a test to be patient or humbled in an issue like this. Sometimes patience is human-directed. Waiting your turn in line or traffic certainly demands patience. Waiting for a teenager to mature can require an extraordinary amount of patience. In any case, whether a stranger is in your way, your coworker is nagging you, or your teenager is going through a period of acute self-righteousness, you must endure discomfort because of other people.

But even more, challenging at times is the patience that is God-directed. In every Christian's life, there comes a time when one must wait upon God. Sometimes we must wait for a need to be met, such as finding a job. Other times we must wait for the satisfaction of a significant desire, like finding a spouse or conceiving a child. At other times we wait for God to fulfill a promise, to comfort us during a trial, or to assure us of our forgiveness for some sin. In these cases, we must be patient with God. Have you ever felt so far off from all of this? Have you forgiven yourself so that God can work and forgive you? It's life, and I always find myself being put through a lesson expressed in the end with a blessing. No matter how hard the outcome, the end will be a learning lesson.

Patience Is Difficult

I don't know which is more complex—exercising patience with God or other human beings. Both can be tremendous challenges, and none of us have perfected the art of being patient with each other or with God. I become impatient with myself (a potential third category worth considering) because I struggle to be patient with others, God, and my current situation! I ask myself in prayer along with God seeking the end, but there is always the starting point knocking at my door, bringing problems & new challenges that makes my faith feel as if it's standing on Rocky grounds.

But patience is challenging in both cases. First, why is patience with other people so difficult? A natural response is, "All human beings are sinners and therefore selfish and annoying." But a psychological explanation also helps to explain why patience is so challenging. It concerns what philosophers call the "egocentric predicament," which is the natural human condition of being immediately aware only of one's thoughts and feelings.

When standing in line or waiting in traffic, for example, all the people waiting are equally as worthy of getting what they are waiting for or arriving at their destinations. However, I know only my thoughts and am intimately aware of only my own needs, which naturally inclines me to put myself first. The result is frustration that I'm not first, which strongly tempts me to be impatient. Have you ever felt the same? Do you feel you should be first at things or put first in the eyes of others?

A second reason patience is such a challenge is that none of us struggle with precisely the same temptations as others. Nor are our particular strengths and weaknesses the same as those of others. One person is even-tempered and can't understand why her friend sometimes flies off the handle. But the person with a bad temper cannot understand how her even-keeled friend can be habitually late to meetings. And both of them get annoyed at a third friend's tendency to overeat.

This is, of course, another aspect of the egocentric predicament. None of these friends knows what it's like to have the others' peculiar weaknesses. Nor does each comprehend how much effort the others are exerting to be as moral as they are, for it's not immediately apparent how hard the others work to control themselves. The result, again, is the temptation to become impatient with them.

Why is patience toward God so difficult? The explanation boils down to our tendency to see things only from our point of view. Further reasons compound the difficulty of waiting upon God. For one thing, patience with God involves faith, and to exercise faith is to surrender absolute control of one's life. To lack faith is to give in to one's desire for control. So our patience with God will only be as vital as our ability to overcome this desire and surrender every aspect of our lives.

Patience with God is a challenge, too, because sometimes it's unclear whether it is God we're waiting for or whether we should even wait on him. The unemployed may wonder, "Have I waited too long rather than taking more action?" The person desiring a spouse might second-guess herself, "Have I taken the right prayer life or enough of not winning or winning or social steps?" And the childless couple might wonder, should we pray more or fast in the Spirit - Should we pursue clinical help to conceive?" Sometimes it's simply unclear whether God wants us to wait or take another action. The mind is always wondering how to get the conflict handled and not delayed in what it's uncomfortable standing in!

Finally, and most difficult of all, there's no guarantee that God will, indeed, act to satisfy our desires. We are standing in. Most situations that demand patience aren't regarding specific promises of God.

Although he has told us he will meet all our needs, he hasn't guaranteed that our desires, even significant ones, will be satisfied.

Here, someone might note the biblical promise that if you *"Delight yourself in the Lord...He will give you the desires of your heart"* (**Ps 37:4**). This, however, is not a promise that all of our present desires will be fulfilled the way we want them to be.

Sometimes they are, but God often keeps this promise by adjusting our desires to bring them to his will. If this is disappointing, keep in mind that even if God does change our desires, they are still our sincere desires! Because we trust him and love him. I had to come to grip's that my faith only sustained me after letting go of myself and putting the patient attitude to work on waiting on God to direct the path of the desires of the new heart I have that brings patience.

Patience Is Developed

It's been said that nothing teaches like experience. To some degree, this is true of the virtues. Pain and suffering teach us endurance and empathy. The experience of mercy and forgiveness inclines us to be more merciful and forgiving. We gain moral maturity each day precisely because each day brings some difficulty that we must overcome. Like it or not, we persevere and are morally better for it. James tells us to *"Consider it pure joy…whenever you face trials of many kinds because you know that the testing of your faith develops perseverance. Perseverance must finish its work so that you may be mature and complete, not lacking anything."* **(James 1:2-4)**

Pampered bodies grow sluggish through sloth, not work but movement, and their weight exhaust them. Prosperity unbruised cannot endure a single blow, but a man who has been in a constant feud with misfortunes acquires skin calloused by suffering; he yields to no evil and, even if he stumbles, carries the fight on upon his knee.

Misfortunes are designed to build virtue in us, and among the virtues gained through difficulty is patience. That family member or work associate who annoys you is God's gift to you to build your patience. That man who is Cyberbullying you on the internet and turning your life upside down is a blessing, not a curse or punishment! If you're stuck with a job you don't like and can't find any other work, God is building your patience. If not, one wants to hire you because of your past or criminal record, it's happening for a reason, and the end of that is a rainbow. Each nuisance, long wait, affliction, mosquito bite, traffic jam, and body ache in the life of the Christian raises your threshold of tolerance ever so much.

Even tedious sermons and difficult reading (perhaps including what you are enduring now!) can make you more patient. Think about all you have faced and seen others face in your family line of those around you suffering. You are not alone or without suffering because everyone will deal with the meaning of life and the unexpected consequences that hit us all here on earth. I had to remind myself of this each time I faced the challenges of predestination and conflict between the Spirit and flesh!

So through the daily grind, the Christian grows morally, improving in virtue through various experiences that we might not even consider morally relevant, much less significant. But we who affirm the sovereignty of God shouldn't be surprised by this moral growth through even incidentals, for we believe God is always at work in the details, always moving to bring us into closer conformity to his image (**Romans 8:28**)

That's not to suggest, however, that we can't slow the process of growth by our response to our daily difficulties. Indeed, a bitter or resentful spirit can stunt moral growth. So we must be attentive and pray for the proper attitude toward all our trials, whether petty or profound. The Holy Spirit will maximize the positive effect of those occasions on our moral-spiritual growth. How do we seem to get there on that level? As I said, it's an actual grind of reading and renewing your mind to follow the Spirit of God!

In addition to life experience and the sort of unplanned training that daily living provides in our sanctification, we can do things to accelerate the process of growth in patience (and in virtue generally). We can take steps of moral self-help. One of these is behavior therapy, a practice once popular among Christians but today is virtually forgotten. It involves intentionally afflicting oneself with an annoying or tedious task expressly to develop patience. I see it as being honest with yourself and taking seriously the life that's given you for your calling. Generally, we want to give in, and no one wants to work hard on this beautiful life and purpose planned for all of us, right? It shall be given if we ask with the right motives. Knock! (The Door shall be opened) Seek! You shall find.

Jesus explained this to us in the book of Matthew on how to go about seeking his will and let he will be done rather than the selfishness of gratification pleasing the self-desires within one's self-righteousness.

We may not see this now, but the more you seek God and focus on his directions for you, you can't lose or feel neglected.

Jesus, the Prince of Peace

1:1-11 Christianity teaches men to be joyful under troubles: such exercises are sent from God's love; trials in the way of duty will brighten our graces now and our crown at last. Let us take care, in times of trial, that patience, and not passion, is set to work in us: whatever is said or done, let patience have the saying and doing of it. When the work of patience is complete, it will furnish all necessary for our Christian race and warfare.

We should not pray so much for the removal of an affliction as for wisdom to use it properly. And who does not want wisdom to guide him under trials, regulating his own Spirit and managing his affairs? Here is something in answer to every discouraging turn of the mind when we go to God under a sense of our weakness and folly. If, after all, any should say, this may be the case with some, but I fear I shall not succeed, the promise is, to any that asketh, it shall be given. A mind with single and prevailing regard to its spiritual and eternal interest that keeps steady in its purposes for God will grow wise by afflictions, continue fervent in devotion, and rise above trials and oppositions. When our faith and spirits rise and fall with second causes, there will be instability in our words and actions. This may not always expose men to contempt, but such ways cannot please God. No condition of life is such as to hinder rejoicing in God. Those of low degree may rejoice if they are exalted to be rich in faith and heirs of the kingdom of God, and the rich may rejoice in humbling providences that lead to a humble and lowly disposition of mind.

Worldly wealth is a withering thing. Then, let him that is rich rejoice in the Grace of God, which makes and keeps him humble, and in the trials and exercises which teach him to seek happiness in and from God, not from perishing enjoyments.

> *"Draw near to God, and he will draw near to you. Cleanse your hands, you sinners, and purify your hearts, you double-minded."*
>
> *- James 4:8*

It means, properly, one who has two souls; then one who is wavering or inconstant. It applies to a man who has no settled principles; is controlled by passion; is influenced by widespread feeling; is now inclined to one opinion or course of conduct, and now to another.

He is unstable in all his ways - That is, not merely regarding prayer, the point particularly under discussion, but in respect to everything. From the instability which the wavering must evince regarding prayer, the apostle makes the general remark concerning such a man that stability and firmness could be expected on no subject. The hesitancy that manifested on that one subject would extend to all, and we might expect to find such a man irresolute and undetermined. This is always true.

If we find a man who takes hold of the promises of God with firmness; who feels the most profound assurance when he prays that God will hear prayer; who always goes to him without hesitation in his perplexities and trials, never wavering, we shall find one who is firm in his principles, steady in his integrity, settled in his determinations, and steadfast in his plans of life - a man whose character we shall feel that we understand, and in whom we can confide. Such a man eminently was Luther, and the Spirit, which is thus displayed by taking firm hold of the promises of God, is the best kind of religion.

How Does a Double-Minded Man Behave?

Based on what James 1 warns readers to avoid, double-minded people fluctuate in their loyalty to Christ. Their belief in whether or not he existed may not shift back and forth, but their commitment to following him changes, sometimes following other gods instead. It is safe to assume that this conflict will create many issues in the double-minded person's life, from increased doubts to struggles with sin.

According to **James 4:7**, we must submit to God and draw near Him. Of course, part of this requires being discerning. As a Christian, it's good to be an investigator and consider what you truly believe. You don't have to take other people's word for everything. However, we find our complete identity in our relationship with God. We will have struggles and doubts.

However, we find our final resting place in his care. Pray and seek a closer relationship with God so that He can discern some of your thoughts concerning peace and direction for a good life without wavering the doubts of being double-minded in your walk.

How Can We Repent from Being Double-Minded?

If you have been double-minded, ask God for forgiveness. You can turn from your old ways and pick up your cross and follow God rather than yourselves. Then begin making chances so you can turn from double-minded to single-minded in your devotion to God. Get in the Word of God. Think about what entertainment you watch, and consider what messages it sends you. Seek music and other entertainment that helps you stay grounded in religious ideas.

If you are in situations where you feel tempted to be double-minded, focus on what the Word of God says about the matter. This will settle an issue. The Word of God gives you peace. Bible says to study God's Word to show thyself approved unto God. A workman that needeth not to be ashamed, rightly dividing the word of truth.

The Bible contains verses that can bring peace amid struggles, worries, and fear. If we ask God, He promises us HIS peace "that passes all understanding"! When we take time to step back from the pressure of life and come into God's presence, He can speak promises of hope and comfort over our circumstances. Use the Bible verses about peace for meditation when you feel overwhelmed and do not know the next step.

The best thing you can do when you are filled with anxiety and worry is to find a quiet place to pray, read Scripture, and listen to encouraging worship music. God wants you to live life to the fullest, including being at peace. You experience the peace of God when you come to Him in humility and accept the blessings He wants for you through Jesus Christ. Here's a sample: *God, I need your peace and healing. Grant me both so I can take heart and face the trial. Help me to press on in the race of life so that I may have peace, God!*

CHAPTER 7: FAITHFULNESS

"If we confess our sins, he is faithful and just to forgive us our sins and to cleanse us from all unrighteousness."

- 1 John 1:9

In our fast-paced, attention-grabbing world, it is easy to get caught up in the daily grind, get distracted, and lose sight of our true purpose in life—the worship and love of God.

Yet we are told to run our race with our eyes focused on Christ: "Let us run with perseverance the race marked out for us, fixing our eyes on Jesus, the pioneer, and perfecter of faith." How can we resist the allure of the world and keep our focus where it belongs, on Christ? This is a daily struggle with the news and everyday life challenges that arise at the top of your day. Sometimes we walk right into fixing the day when we should be fixated on the race in doing God's will.

I always had this issue with maintaining the proper steps to focus my mind on the steps I should be walking. I instead listen to or hear the wrong voices to walk the race, thinking that someone else will run it for me. That was my thinking back then, and I still fall short of this command to run the race! My focus was deemed and slow paste for sure. I needed faithfulness in something that would keep me grounded and rooted to stay strong.

To focus is to direct one's attention or concentrate on something. If we are focused on Christ, He has our attention; we are concentrating on Him and His word; He occupies the forefront of our minds. Such a focus is only fitting because Jesus "is the head of the body, the church; he is the beginning and the firstborn from among the dead so that in everything he might have the supremacy" (**Colossians 1:8**). By rights, He should be our focus. Nothing else should be ahead of this at all.

What can help us stay focused on Christ? Since then, you have been raised with Christ, set your hearts on things above, where Christ is, seated at the right hand of God. Set your mind on things above, not on earthly things. You died, and your life is now hidden with Christ in God. When Christ, who is your life, appears, you will also appear with him in glory." We are to focus on "things above," remembering that Christ is seated in the place of glory and power. The command is also given because we have been raised to new life with Christ. To focus on the things above, we must consciously remove our focus from "earthly things," and the reason is given - we have died to self, and Christ is our very life. Helping us stay focused on Christ reminds us that Jesus is coming again, and when we see Him, we will know him.

God had done so much for all of us; why should we leave him out of ourselves, walk without faithfulness, and stay focused on his true desires for our lives?

Some of the things that Christ has done or is doing for us is a blessing because He shared our humanity. He breaks the power of the devil, and He frees us! He is our "merciful and faithful high priest" who suffered for us and helped those tempted in this world. Because of all this, **Hebrews 3:1** says, "*Therefore, holy brothers and sisters, who share in the heavenly calling, fix your thoughts on Jesus, whom we acknowledge as our apostle and high priest.*"

Here are some practical ways for a born-again believer in staying focused on Christ:

Commit to reading the Bible. A believer can't be consistent in the world without having his attention drawn again and again to Christ. The Scriptures point to me that I am doing wrong and falling into a sinful zone when I should be walking the steps of Jesus and not causing myself danger or developing bad habits into darkness.

Develop your prayer life. If you want to know how to pray, read Jesus' instructions to His disciples in **Luke 11:1-14**: As you speak to the Lord throughout your day, you will naturally be more focused on Him and not yourself. Little things, big things—we can come to the Lord with all of our cares. The command is to "pray continually" and to always be in an attitude and atmosphere of instant prayer.

Trust the Lord as your only protector. "My eyes are ever on the LORD, for only he will release my feet from the snare"! Once we understand the spiritual dangers we face daily, we will focus more on Christ, our one and only Savior, who has the power of deliverance.

Recognize your need and the Lord as the source of all good things. "Behold, as the eyes of servants look to the hand of their master, as the eyes of a maidservant to the hand of her mistress, so our eyes look to the LORD our God, till he has mercy upon us." (**Psalms 123:1**) The world offers various means of obtaining love, joy, and peace, but they are destined to disappoint. As believers, we need to understand that love, joy, and peace (and a myriad of other fine gifts) are the direct result of our relationship with Christ (**Galatians 5:22**) is the truth and nothing but the truth!

See the world for what it is—a sin-filled place of desperate need. The darker the world is to us, the more the light of Christ will stand out. It's not hard to focus on a light in a darkened room. "We . . . have the prophetic message as something completely reliable, and you will do well to pay attention to it, as to a light shining in a dark place, until the day dawns and the morning star rises in your hearts". Those who stay focused on Christ will find their perspective on worldly things changing. As I said, I had to find the hard way to see this light in a dark room. Turn your eyes upon Jesus, / Look full in His wonderful face, / And the things of earth will grow strangely dim / In the light of His glory and grace."

We can't afford to be out of touch with this calling in our lives because rejecting his calling is dangerous. We have to be alert and ready for the morning to the night, redeeming the time because the days are evil, and the hearts of all of us can be so deceitful and reject the faith of what we are all to be called to do God's goodwill.

Here I am—the man supposed to have it all together. After all, I wrote the book and others out there. I should be as strong as Samson and as obedient as Jesus. No battle should take me down. I should be like a mountain, immovable by every monsoon.

But I am not; the reality is: I still get shaken, unsure, and a little nervous. Bloggers are attacking me, and those who hate and are jealous can make you feel drained and unsure! I'm feeling unstoppable now, and it lifted my heart higher to see and have faith in my work.

It's embarrassing to say that despite my 90% growth, I still live with a 10% lack. Friends, the pride in me doesn't want you to see me this way. I want to hide the embarrassing parts of me in my bedroom, shut the door on it, and return to the world as strong and mighty. But that would be a lie. We all have weaknesses, and Easy to fall as straightforward to walk right into sin! It's always knocking at the door, and that door is the heart of desire and winning!

The reality is: I don't know it all, my friends. In many ways, I fail. On my own, I fail. By my strength, I fail. When I control, I fail.

Do you feel like you are failing? Failing those around you? Failing to do faith well? Failing to find answers? Failing to make way for those you love? Failing to be pure, honest, and true to God? Failing to surrender? Failing. Failing. Failing. Life seems like a roller coaster, and your mind is going crazy!

What if…today, you let the weight of your super-sized backpack full of bricks go? What if you began to speak a new word and release new life? Just back up from the cares of life, adjust your backpack, and clean out all the garbage? It's easier said than done.

We must be honest with ourselves for proper rest and solid grounds to walk on! I believe we should all have this type of voice ourselves.

It sounds like this "Father God, the enemy accuser is right. I have (controlled, grasped, managed, and not let go of the reigns, put your words here). I am sorry; forgive me."

This is powerful because rather than trying to defend ourselves against the inner attacks we know are true, we release them to God. The second we acknowledge we are wrong, we see how Jesus is 100 % correct, righteous, and proper by our side, ready to restore us. He is not undone by what He knows we've done; He is coming to release us from the inner turmoil of it. He has done this for me in a time of crying out and asking him for hope and a future. While we were still sinners, Christ died for us. (**1 Pet. 5:8**)

While you and I sin – Christ comes for us.

Why? What is Jesus' plan in all this?

> *"And the God of all grace, who called you to his eternal glory in Christ, after you have suffered a little while, will himself restore you and make you strong, firm and steadfast."*

> *- 1 Pet. 5:10*

He comes to restore us, to make us strong and steadfast. He does not come to shame, hate, or criticize us. The path to Jesus always leads to freedom.

Friends, rest assured, whether it is me, Mother Theresa, Billy Graham, or you – there is no perfect keeper of God's law. There is no key to sudden perfection. There is no way to the freedom of life—to grace, either—except Jesus.

He has designed our faith walk in some ways (or the fall of Adam and Eve has) to be a continual return. We keep coming home. We keep coming back. We keep getting up. We keep surrounding ourselves with His truth.

We need strategies, wisdom, truth, and promises lined up in their fanny-pack like weapons for hard days. We are practiced with thought patterns of God's love so that when defeat shows up, we don't listen to it. We are equipped with little tips on how to change bad habits and how to embrace Godly vision. We know how to fight proactively rather than respond reactively. The world doesn't rule us; we inhabit but are ruled by God's love for us, which helps us love the world. We don't get with God once, but we are so full of desire we keep coming back to the well of His love. We believe in God's love for them. We hope and see His best. We walk by faith and not by sight.

We see how far we have come. We now see the good, yet we don't run from the bad. We bring it to Jesus.

I had to bring everything to him, good and bad! Life is so much easier with confession, knowing who to face with your life struggles, and being faithful.

"Battle ready is helping me understand what I mean to God. It is helping me understand what I mean to God. I'm beginning to understand I'm precious to Him."

This makes me feel not alone in this fight or struggle!

Before responding, seek God's guidance.

> *"And Jehoshaphat feared, and set himself to seek the LORD, and proclaimed a fast throughout all Judah. And Judah gathered themselves together, to ask help of the LORD: even out of all the cities of Judah they came to seek the LORD."*
>
> *- 2 Chronicles 20:3-6*

Before any plan was made, before he ran to any counselor, Jehoshaphat sought the Lord. Acknowledge that God is in control.

"O LORD, God of our fathers, are you not the God who is in heaven? You rule over all the kingdoms of the nations. Power and might are in your hand, and no one can withstand you."

The enemies weren't driving the circumstance. They had no authority over God's people. No matter how dire our circumstances are, God is sovereign. Remember God's faithfulness and promises.

"O our God, did you not drive out the inhabitants of this land before your people Israel and give it forever to the descendants of Abraham, your friend? They have lived in it and have built in it a sanctuary for your Name, saying, 'If calamity comes upon us, whether the sword or judgment or plague or famine, we will stand in your presence before this temple that bears your Name and will cry out to you in our distress, and you will hear us and save us.'"

Each new trial can cause a new crisis of belief for us. Remembering how God has already worked on our behalf bolsters our faith during trials.

In the heat of the battle, whisper to your soul that God did not take you this far to drop you now. Admit utter dependence on God.

"For we have no power to face this vast army attacking us. We do not know what to do, but our eyes are upon you.'"

Have you ever been in a place where you had no answer and could only look to God?

That's a place of utter dependence on God. Don't miss that God — acting in perfect love — had allowed Judah to reach a place of utter dependence on him.

Why? Maybe because when we are utterly dependent on God, we learn to trust him more than ever. And with our eyes on God, we see him more than ever. That's where we find Judah.

"This is what the LORD says: 'Do not be afraid or discouraged because of this vast army. For the battle is not yours, but God's.'"

God allowed Judah to come face-to-face with a battle too hard for them and then revealed this foundational truth. Though spoken explicitly to Judah, it's a Biblical principle that applies to all of God's children.

Praise God. We could stop here and have enough meat to feed on for days. But let's keep going because what God does next is jaw-dropping.

"Tomorrow, march down against them. They will climb up by the Pass of Ziz, and you will find them at the end of the gorge in the Desert of Jeruel. You will not have to fight this battle. Take up your positions; stand firm and see the deliverance the LORD will give you, O Judah and Jerusalem. Do not be afraid; do not be discouraged. Go face them tomorrow, and the LORD will be with you."

The battle was the Lord's, but they didn't get to stay home in bed.

In faith, Judah had to march out, take up positions and stand firm before seeing how God would deliver beyond their wildest imagination.

"Jehoshaphat bowed with his face to the ground, and all the people of Judah and Jerusalem fell in worship before the LORD."

What had changed? The dark clouds of a gathering enemy still loomed, but Israel had traded fear for faith, ushering in praise.

The Truth When You're Facing a Battle

When we're facing a battle too big for us, we need to anchor ourselves in the faithfulness and power of God. Since God has allowed the battle, ultimately, the battle is not ours. The battle is the Lord's.

One of the most stunning chapters where God demonstrates this is **2 Chronicles 20.**

This chapter came up in my daily Bible reading when I dreaded the one-year mark of my best friend's death and was fighting fear and loneliness, financial issues, and parenting struggles. Even the broken lawnmower felt like an enemy. I felt as if everyone or everything was against me or not for me at all.

I needed the powerful reminder in **2 Chronicles 20** that God fights for me. He fights for you, too. We must be reminded daily that it will take God to calm the storm and bring a rainbow the morning we open our eyes to life's vantage, struggles, and challenges. Joy always comes in the mornings, as the Bible tells us!

If you're facing a battle and need reminding of your all-mighty, always-faithful God, buckle up to dive into this chapter!

First, look at the overwhelming battle Judah faced in Chapter 20.

King Jehoshaphat, who ruled Judah, is regarded as a "good king." He had worked hard to turn Judah from its idol worship back to God. Yet, despite following hard after God, he suddenly faced an unprovoked war from three neighboring countries who'd allied together to obliterate Judah. In **2 Chronicles 20**, Judah becomes surrounded by these enemies.

"Some men came and told Jehoshaphat, 'A vast army is coming against you from Edom... it is already in Hazazon Tamar!'"

How did King Jehoshaphat respond?

Unlike so many ungodly kings, he could have grumbled that he was facing a battle when he obeyed God.

He could have rallied his troops, planned a strategic counterattack, and reinforced the border.

He could even have panicked.

But he did none of these. Here's how King Jehoshaphat did respond and what we can learn about facing our battles.

"Alarmed, Jehoshaphat resolved to inquire of the LORD and proclaimed a fast for all Judah. The people of Judah came together to seek help from the LORD; indeed, they came from every town in Judah to seek him."

Before any plan was made, before he ran to any counselor, we all have to seek the Lord.

Acknowledge that God is in control.

"O LORD, God of our fathers, are you not the God who is in heaven? You rule over all the kingdoms of the nations. Power and might are in your hand, and no one can withstand you."

The enemies weren't driving the circumstance. They had no authority over God's people. No matter how dire our circumstances are, God is sovereign. Remember God's faithfulness and promises.

"O our God, did you not drive out the inhabitants of this land before your people Israel and give it forever to the descendants of Abraham, your friend? They have lived in it and have built in it a sanctuary for your Name, saying, 'If calamity comes upon us, whether the sword or judgment or plague or famine, we will stand in your presence before this temple that bears your Name and will cry out to you in our distress, and you will hear us and save us."

Each new trial can cause a new crisis of belief for us. Remembering how God has already worked on our behalf bolsters our faith during trials.

In the heat of the battle, whisper to your soul that God did not take you this far to drop you now.

Admit utter dependence on God.

"For we have no power to face this vast army attacking us. We do not know what to do, but our eyes are upon you."

Have you ever been in a place where you had no answer and could only look to God? But at times, don't feel him around your issue at all? It's so mind-boggling to have this cold impression of being alone. Now he aims to let you know he is there and ready to help you focus on faithfulness.

That's a place of utter dependence on God. Don't miss that God — acting in perfect love — had allowed Judah to reach a place of utter dependence on him.

Why? Maybe because when we are utterly dependent on God, we learn to trust him more than ever. And with our eyes on God, we see him more than ever. That's where we find Judah.

"This is what the LORD says: Do not be afraid or discouraged because of this vast army. For the battle is not yours, but God's."

God allowed Judah to come face-to-face with a battle too hard for them and then revealed this foundational truth. Though spoken explicitly to Judah, it's a Biblical principle that applies to all of God's children.

Praise God. He will speak to us and control the issue if we let him fight for us.

The difficulty comes in all shapes and sizes. Sometimes the difficulty isn't a drastic tragedy but the busy chaos of managing life.

With all that we want to accomplish weekly and daily, we can end up worn out, disappointed, and never feeling like we've finished anything. My to-do list feels like it goes on forever.

One of my friend's mother was one of those amazingly talented people who seemed to be able to do it all. She was a leader, a judge, a prophetess, a wife, and a mother. And along with that, she courageously led her people into battle. Though phenomenally inspirational, her life can leave me feeling like I can't relate. How did she do it all? We wonder how others seem to do it right. We watch the actions of others and see the power in them that carries the load of challenge & desires to push through hardship as if it's normal for them, and they take it with a smile on their face!

Every day we work demanding jobs and do what we can to help care for our families. We might not have the title she did, but life demands a lot from us each day: settling disputes and helping people with marriages, finances, kids, and health. We all struggle and feel like giving up, right?

Her family (the people of Israel) had its dysfunctions just like many of ours do. Hers was just bigger. We can look to her as an example of how to handle the chaos of our daily lives.

Just like Deborah said to Barak, in the Bible…. Then Deborah said to Barak, *"Go! This is the day the Lord has given Sisera into your hands. Has not the Lord gone ahead of you?" So Barak went down Mount Tabor, with ten thousand men following him. 15 At Barak's advance, the Lord routed Sisera and all his chariots and army by the sword, and Sisera got down from his chariot and fled on foot."*

Judges 4:14-15 NIV

Remember this verse in the Bible?

Deborah believed and trusted God in a way that can be hard for us to do. God was real and present in her life. She believed that victory was already hers through God.

If I had this strong a belief that God's hand was in every effort of my day, I would be a lot more content with each day's accomplishments. I could then relax and know God fights all my battles. I wouldn't be so overwhelmed by my busy schedule, but I can handle it because God is on my side.

Deborah described herself as a "mother" to Israel. We can learn from this: Deborah cared about the people she led and, as a mother, cared for her children. She was motivated to serve no matter the demands because she cared about the people. Not about the title or accomplishments but about caring for others.

When I get overwhelmed or worn out, I want to quit; thinking about others I care about – my friends, family, and neighborhood- helps me keep going.

Deborah was a great example of this. She had become their mother, and that relationship helped her to keep going.

- What are the areas of your life that overwhelm you the most?
- What is one thing that you could do to make God more of a part of your daily life?
- Who is someone that you could reach out to and help this week?

Zechariah & Elizabeth: Trusting God when a longing is unfulfilled

A longing unfulfilled can be disheartening. Imagine having been married for a long time, being unable to have kids, and living in a culture that measured God's love for you by the number of children you have. This is the story of Zechariah and Elizabeth, a couple described as "very old" and "childless." Can you imagine being in their situation? We must focus on being humbled because we could get worse off than we are.

They are an example of people who understood longing unfulfilled; the heartache of being denied something you long for and not knowing why.

Have you been denied something you've longed for a long time? Maybe it's a lingering health situation that won't go away, a child who rejects your influence, a character weakness you cannot overcome, or a sin that plagues you and your relationships. Zechariah and Elizabeth understand. They also understand how to remain faithful while waiting on God. This is a struggle we all have, and once we turn to God, it's his issue, not mine, correct?

In the time of Herod, king of Judea, there was a priest named Zechariah, who belonged to the priestly division of Abijah; his wife Elizabeth was also a descendant of Aaron. Both were righteous in the sight of God, blamelessly observing all the Lord's commands and decrees. But they were childless because Elizabeth could not conceive, and they were both ancient.

> *"But the angel reassured him, "Don't fear, Zachariah. Your prayer has been heard. Elizabeth, your wife, will bear a son by you. You are to name him John. You're going to leap like a gazelle for joy, and not only you—many will delight in his birth. He'll achieve great stature with God. "He'll drink neither wine nor beer. He'll be filled with the Holy Spirit from the moment he leaves his mother's womb. He will turn many sons and daughters of Israel back to their God. He will herald God's arrival in the style and strength of Elijah, soften the hearts of parents to children, and kindle devout understanding among hardened skeptics—he'll get the people ready for God."*

> *- Luke 1:13-15a-15b-17*

> *And he will go on before the Lord, in the spirit and power of Elijah, to turn the hearts of the parents to their children and the disobedient to the wisdom of the righteous—to prepare a people prepared for the Lord."*

> *- Luke 1:5-7,13-14,16-17 NIV*

What inspires me about Zechariah and Elizabeth is their ability to trust God amid an unfulfilled longing. We know they trusted God because they continued to serve God, and God described them as righteous.

The angel showed up to Zechariah with good news while Zechariah was serving God as a priest. He could have given up on God but decided to keep serving God despite his unfulfilled longing.

How do you handle adversity? If you are like me and endure adversity for any length, losing faith and quickly turning to self-pity and unbelief can be easy. This leads us to quit praying and expecting God to move.

The story of Zechariah and Elizabeth is about the faithfulness of God and what it means to

God showed his faithfulness with Zechariah and Elizabeth by working to bless their lives even after they waited a long time. When I have to wait, I get distracted or want to give up. It's a weakening of the flesh that causes us all to feel times of pressure or whatever is keeping us back from moving forward.

Secondly, Zechariah and Elizabeth lived by faith with the conviction that God loved them and wanted to bless them. They wanted to stay righteous while waiting for their longings to be fulfilled.

When we experience waiting periods, we can have hope by remembering God's faithfulness and choosing to live by faith.

Reflecting:

- What are you longing for?
- Are you honest with yourself, others, and God about your longings?
- Have you quit believing God hears you and wants to bless you?

Isaiah: trusting God through bad news

God chose Isaiah to deliver an important message to the Israelites. God set up His people for a great future of redemption and hope.

But before all that could happen, God gave Isaiah an intense vision that overwhelmed him. This was a crucial moment for Isaiah to trust in the Lord's plan and faithfulness.

> *My stomach sinks. My gut churns with pain. I can hardly bear the news as a woman in labor wrenches and writhes. I cannot hear because I'm bent over in agony. I cannot see because I'm deep in the fog of depression.*
>
> *- Isaiah 21:3 VOICE*

One of my biggest fears is the fear of bad news. For me, the bad news is usually followed by worst-case scenario thinking and suddenly being overtaken by anxiety and feelings of helplessness.

During these times, prayer can be complicated. My flesh finds relief in making a plan or figuring out a solution, but I learned that going through difficulty is an opportunity to transform my prayer life.

Often I harden my pain by minimizing and hiding it. I get annoyed and even offended when friends try to help me. My resistance to vulnerability makes me unsympathetic and fake. Isaiah is inspiring because he doesn't hold back from God. He expresses his deep pain and how hard it is to hear and see Him in the midst of it all. His connection to God deepens during difficulties.

He said, "You are my servant, Israel, and you will bring me glory." I replied, "But my work seems so useless! I have spent my strength for nothing and no purpose. Yet I leave it all in the LORD's hand; I will trust God for my reward."

- Isaiah 49:3-4 NLT

If we could be like this and accept this battle as God allowed it to be in one life like Isaiah, we could grow so strong and mighty as if we have the power to do anything.

I think Isaiah's faith stayed strong despite awful news because he was honest about his doubt and frustration, and he believed sincerely in God's purpose. Believing that God chose me to help others know Him challenges and inspire me. Our vulnerable prayers unlock a deeper level of intimacy with God.

Reflecting again:

- Are you honest with God about the depths of your pain? Hopelessness, confusion, anger, depression?
- Have you found yourself slipping into the dark shadows? Isolating, negative thinking, unbelief, and loss of passion toward God.

- How does terrible news affect your relationship with God? Do you cry out more or avoid Him?

Woman healed by Jesus: trusting God is taking risks despite the pain

In **Mark 5**, we find a prevalent scene throughout the gospels: a large crowd has gathered around Jesus. People from all over the region rushed to him and pressed against him. In the crowd was a woman suffering from chronic bleeding for 12 years.

She had visited many doctors and had spent all she had on treatments. But instead of getting better, her condition worsened. Because of the nature of her illness, she was considered unclean according to the laws and traditions of the time. She was sick, broke, and an outcast.

Yet because of her confident faith in Jesus, she could ignore the pain for a moment and ultimately take the risk that changed everything.

> *When she heard about Jesus, she came up behind him in the crowd and touched his cloak because she thought, "If I just touch his clothes, I will be healed." Immediately her bleeding stopped, and she felt free from her suffering. At once, Jesus realized that power had gone out from him. He turned around in the crowd and asked, "Who touched my clothes?"*
>
> *"You see the people crowding against you," his disciples answered, "and yet you can ask, 'Who touched me?' "But Jesus kept looking around to see who had done it. Then the woman, knowing what had happened to her, came and fell at his feet and, trembling with fear, told him the whole truth. He said to her, "Daughter, your faith has healed you. Go in peace and be freed from your suffering."*
>
> *- Mark 5:27-34 NIV*

If we can only taste and see or feel Jesus in everyday life, what a relief and joy to know he is there for all our doubts and fears that overtake us. We get so loaded with life challenges, and testing daily to find a way to who we are can be very disconnected and discouraging.

Trying something new may be the last thing on your mind, especially when you have a chronic health challenge or are amid long-standing troubles. We have been trying to start a family for the past few years at first dating, my soon-to-be wife. It's been a grueling series of doctor appointments and tests that have left us frustrated and forgotten. We thought we could not have any children or that it was the way God wanted it! One day she walked into the house from teaching classes, yelling and saying I'm pregnant! It was something so out of our control to happen. God blessed us with a little girl and, finally, a family. The best day of my life, but very nervous and excited at the same time hearing the news. It's a lot of bible verses that inspire us to believe and see it for what it is!

Although the woman in this passage was unnamed, her story of faith is unforgettable and inspires me never to give up. She took a risk to believe in Jesus and his power. She stepped out of the shadows, made her way through the crowd, and told the whole truth to get closer to Jesus.

When it feels like things will never change, I realize there is.

Tests, pressure, setbacks, failure, and trouble can expose the condition of our faith. We need Bible verses about resilience to help us believe those challenges don't have to own us.

We get stuck wanting our way, and I miss what God is doing and the doors He is opening. Lately, I've seen God create opportunities to build closeness in my marriage, make new friends, and comfort those around me. Seeing God move through my struggles has helped my faith grow.

Reflecting is good to look back and ask yourself these questions:

- Does your health (physical or mental/emotional) affect your faith? How do you respond when things don't go well?
- How has your faith been affected by a long-standing difficult situation? Be honest with yourself, God, and your friends.
- What by faith can you do that might feel risky?

Moses: trusting God when there is no way out

Difficult times can lead us to a point where we feel like our backs are against the wall, and there are minimal options before us to find a way out or a solution to overcome. We are left wondering, "How did I get myself here?" When I was hospitalized for COVID-19's deadly movement a couple of years back, I couldn't move. I was in pain constantly. How did I get myself here?" What happens? I kept asking myself, laying there in so much pain and agony with tears rolling down my eyes, thinking I would soon die and catch the viruses we all wanted to ignore and stay away from.

When God is calling you to face a challenge or something to stronger your faith, it will happen no matter how much you don't want it to appear in your life. So many thoughts were going through my mind at that moment, and it was fear - but God had taken control and given me faith to overcome my emotions at heart that were getting in the way of my healing. We seem frustrated when our feelings and emotions get in the way of our faith!

I discovered I needed to shift my thinking and see this setback as a set-up for God to move. Moses experienced that feeling when, after leading Israel out of Egypt, they were stuck between the Red Sea and an angry Egyptian army. The moment between God, Moses, and the Israelites.

Pharaoh will say of the Israelites, 'They are wandering in the land; the wilderness has shut them in.' I will harden (make stubborn, defiant) Pharaoh's heart so that he will pursue them; and I will be glorified and honored through Pharaoh and all his army, and the Egyptians shall know [without any doubt] and acknowledge that I am the LORD." And they did so.

The Egyptians chased them with all the horses and war chariots of Pharaoh, his horsemen, and his army, and they overtook them as they camped by the sea, beside Pi-hahiroth, in front of Baal-zephon.

Then Moses said to the people, "Do not be afraid! Take your stand [be firm and confident and undismayed] and see the salvation of the LORD which He will accomplish for you today; for those Egyptians whom you have seen today, you will never see again. The LORD will

fight for you while you [only need to] keep silent and remain calm."
We can't seem to admit that if we let God in and handle the daily
battles, we would be confident and brave through life dealings.

> *"The LORD said to Moses, 'Why do you cry to Me? Tell
> the sons of Israel to move forward [toward the sea]. As
> for you, lift your staff, stretch out your hand over the sea,
> and divide it so that the sons of Israel may go through the
> middle of the sea on dry land.*
>
> *As for Me, hear this: I will harden the hearts of the
> Egyptians, and they will go in [the sea] after them, and
> I will be glorified and honored through Pharaoh and all
> his army, and his war chariots and his horsemen. And the
> Egyptians shall know [without doubt] and acknowledge
> that I am the LORD when I am glorified and honored
> through Pharaoh, his war chariots, and his charioteers.'"*
>
> *- Exodus 14:3-4,9,13-18 AMP*

God guided the Israelites to the exact place he wanted them to be,
right on the edge of the Red Sea. With the water at their backs and
Pharaoh and the Egyptians bearing down on them, only God could
provide a way for it.

This experience can occur in our lives from time to time. We feel
like we are in an impossible situation just for God to show us how
powerful he is.

CHAPTER 8: GENTLENESS

"Put on then, as God's chosen ones, holy and beloved, compassion, kindness, lowliness, meekness, and patience."

- Col 3:12

The Bible urges followers of Jesus to be gentle. Not only is it a fruit of the Spirit, but it is also a command in Colossians, Proverbs, and other books. Even Jesus describes himself as "gentle and lowly in heart" in **Matthew 11:29**.

What does it mean to be gentle? Gentleness is similar to kindness, but it involves cultivating a softness of heart toward other people. I get so frustrated when others are not so gentle or nice.

I remember this lady that cut me off in front of traffic on my way to work, and all of a sudden, she gave me the finger as if I did something terrible or cut her off, and it gave her the satisfaction to give me a taste of her mind.

It was a simple mistake, and should we get persecuted for any mistakes against others.

Often, it's all a misunderstanding or communication when these types of things happen.

It was tough not to get even, vindictive, or angry because I would only give back what the enemy wanted. We must be alert and know that the days are evil and temptation is always lurking around the corner for us to grab hold of. Let's say I had given in to this fight with this lady in traffic and gave her a sense of my anger, not knowing it would cause me remorse or repentance later.

I did feel later that I was not gentle or a man of Godly character. It seems that in the long run, after it took place, I had come to my senses and realized I was wrong. Even though she had done what she did to tempt me, it was not my intention to give her a Taste of my mind. It was my flesh wanting to ware back with her fighting the devil with evil, trying to show her I could do better at what she started. In the end, I fell because it was only hurting me. We all have stumbling blocks ahead of us that are constantly causing us to stumble. We never know what someone is going through or why they do what they do to cause those around them to stumble.

"For though the righteous fall seven times, they rise again, but the wicked stumble when calamity strikes."

- Proverbs 24:16

Today we continue to see our sins as wrong and try to change the direction of falling. The character of the Christian as we are and called to be; we are exploring how the various character qualifications of elders are God's calling on all Christians like ourselves.

While elders are meant to exemplify these traits, all Christians are to exhibit them. I want us to consider whether we are displaying these traits and learn how to pray to have them more significantly. We need to look at what it takes or gives to be gentle. Believe me, and it is not always easy to consider these traits valuable in our daily walk without falling short of God's Grace! I struggle daily with being gentle and showing compassion. Why do we turn it on and off? Let's find out why these decisions occur in the saints' walk. My walk is tested daily with the order in the Spirit of God. I highly recommend Paul's teaching because he is an excellent example of explaining in the word how we should be reminded.

Paul writes to Timothy, "*Therefore an overseer must [be] not violent but gentle, not quarrelsome*" (**1 Timothy 3:2–3**). Similarly, he tells Titus that an overseer "must not be arrogant or quick-tempered … or violent" (**Titus 1:7**). The positive characteristic here is gentleness, which is opposed by the two negative characteristics of violence and quarreling. The elder (and, therefore, every mature Christian) pursues gentleness and flees from violence and bickering.

To be gentle is to be tender, humble, and fair, to know what posture and response are fitting for any occasion. It indicates graciousness, a desire to extend mercy to others, and a desire to yield to God's will and other people's preferences. Such gentleness will be expressed first in the home and only subsequently in the church. It is a rare trait, but one we know and love when we see and experience it.

To pursue gentleness is to imitate Jesus. He writes, "Jesus tells us who He is as a person: He is gentle and humble. Too many religious leaders, however, are neither gentle nor humble. They are controlling and proud. They use people to satisfy their fat egos. But Jesus is refreshingly different. He truly loves people, selflessly serving and giving His life for them. He expects His followers—especially the elders who lead His people—to be humble and gentle like Himself."

Similarly, this [gentleness] is the opposite of combative or belligerent. He should not be harsh or mean-spirited. He should be inclined to tenderness and resort to toughness only when the circumstances commend this form of love. His words should not be acid or divisive but helpful and encouraging." We always seem to need to give others a taste of our anger on our shoulders! We need to stop and think twice before reacting because being slow to anger and wrathful will let you see wiser and not let the sun go down on your anger. The Bible speaks on being slow to wrath and slows to speak!

(**Ephesians 4:26**) says, *26 "In your anger do not sin: Do not let the sun go down while you are still angry, 27 and do not give the devil a foothold."*

Paul gets practical in the latter half of the letter to the Ephesians. In this section, he encourages believers to tell the truth to each other, be angry without sinning, stop stealing, work so they can give to others in need, use their words to edify others, not grieve the Holy Spirit, put away sins such as anger, be kind to others, and forgive others just as God has forgiven them.

We have the command to "be angry, and yet do not sin." This statement probably references **Psalm 4:4**, "Tremble and do not sin."

This psalm is sometimes titled "**A Night Prayer**" or "**An Evening Prayer of Trust in God**." Verse 4 continues, "When you are on your beds, search your hearts and be silent." Perhaps this part of the psalm was meant to help the prayerful reader resolve any anger issues in the heart before going to bed. Paul uses this Old Testament passage as a springboard for his command to "not let the sun go down on your anger."

Anger itself is not a sin, but how we use it determines whether it is sinful. Legitimate sin or injustice can be productive. Jesus exhibited righteous anger at times, most notably when He cleaned out His Father's house and the temple (**John 2:13**). But, more often than not, anger becomes sinful because our selfish interests and pride motivate it. Someone or something offends us, and we lash out, just like the lady that cut me off. We end up saying and doing things that we ought not to. Anger rooted in our sinfulness is dangerous and destructive to others and ourselves. We must pay close attention to ourselves when we get out of control or step backward in backsliding in the faith we claim.

One thing that can turn anger into a sinful attitude is to allow it to continue to fester instead of acting on it honestly. Our appeal is not to let the sun go down on our anger or, as the NIV says, "Do not let the sun go down while you are still angry." To allow a period of anger to be unreasonably prolonged is to "give the devil a foothold" it's a blessing knowing we have the Bible to give us order and directions to react upon.

The Bible has many warnings against the improper use of anger. In the same chapter, as we are told not to let the sun go down on our anger, we have a command to put away anger.

James commands us to be "*quick to listen, slow to speak and slow to become angry*" (**James 1:19**). I have repeatedly said this earlier, but it's a reminder that we need to renew our minds daily with verses Paul writes, "Refrain from anger and turn from wrath; do not fret—it leads only to evil." Solomon adds his wisdom: "*Do not be quickly provoked in your spirit, for anger resides in the lap of fools.*"

The book of Proverbs echoes the cautions about anger: "Whoever is patient has great understanding, but one who is quick-tempered displays folly." (**Proverbs 14:29**) and "Good sense makes one slow to anger, and it is his glory to overlook an offense." (**Proverbs 19:11**) we need always to do this and be the better person. The Spirit of a man will always do what's God's way than his way!

We can begin practicing patience in our relationships as we understand why we should be slow to anger. James taught believers to listen to God's Word and put it into practice. He said, *"My dear brothers and sisters, take note of this: Everyone should be quick to listen, slow to speak and slow to become angry, because human anger does not produce the righteousness that God desires. Therefore, get rid of all moral filth and the evil that is so prevalent and humbly accept the word planted in you, which can save you."*

A wise Christian listens to God and obeys and listens to others, carefully considers what he hears, and then answers with cautiously chosen words.

We all have human anger! Don't get it wrong because we still have this anger and must deal with it. James explained that it was a waste of energy. It is motivated by selfishness and ambition and creates division among brothers and sisters in Christ. Anger won't produce the righteousness that God desires: *"Pure and genuine religion in the sight of God the Father means caring for orphans and widows in their distress and refusing to let the world corrupt you." (James 3:27)* tell us.

Anger must be controlled, and we should never use it to sin. If we become angry, we should deal with the anger, and its root quickly and promptly put it away from our lives. We should strive to "keep short accounts" and forgive those we need to forgive promptly—before the sun goes down. If we hold on to anger, we run the risk of bitterness and resentfulness, which provide the devil with a foothold in our lives.

I have learned that unchecked anger among believers will break fellowship and damage the church. We must be careful to heed the closing appeal of Paul's teaching and advice - Be kind and compassionate to one another, forgiving each other, just as in Christ, God forgave you! Christian man and woman elder must be gentle and able to control their temper and respond to others when he is attacked, maligned, and finds themselves in tense or difficult situations. He is marked by patience, tenderness, and a sweet spirit. Negatively, he must not lose control either physically or verbally. He must not respond to others with physical force or threats of violence. When it comes to his words, he must not quarrel or bicker or be one who loves to argue. Even when pushed and exasperated, he will not lash out with his words; he will not crush a bruised reed or snuff out a faintly burning wick. We all fail these tests at times and even practice them.

I am sure you realize that God calls all Christians—not just elders—to be gentle. Elders must serve as examples of gentleness, but we must display this trait to imitate our Savior. There are many texts we can turn to, including this one which tells us that gentleness is a necessary fruit of the Spirit: *"But the fruit of the Spirit is love, joy, peace, patience, kindness, goodness, faithfulness, gentleness, self-control; against such things there is no law."* (**Galatians 5:22-23**).

Shortly after that, Paul says, *"Brothers, if someone is caught in a sin, you who are spiritual should restore him gently."* (**Galatians 6:1**). We want to see the world like ourselves, don't we? We want to change the world and love Jesus to be in everyone's heart for these traits of the fruits of the nine spiritual blessings.

He urges the Christians in Ephesus to walk in a manner worthy of the calling to which they have been called" and says that this involves living "with all humility and gentleness, with patience, bearing with one another in love, eager to maintain the unity of the Spirit in the bond of peace" (**Ephesians 4:1-3**).

When speaking of the congregation under Titus' care, he says, *"Remind them to be under the control of magistrates and authorities,* to be obedient, to be open to every good enterprise."* (**Titus 3:1–2**). The evidence is clear: We are to be gentle to serve as a display of the one who deals so gently with us.

Self-Evaluation

So, how about you? Does your life reflect the meekness and humility of gentleness? I encourage you to ask yourself questions like these prayerfully:

When someone wrongs you, are you prone to lash out in anger? Does that anger express itself physically, verbally, or both? You can't let others' anger cause you to stumble as I did over the misunderstanding with the lady being upset in her car and letting me have it! Are people afraid to confront sin because they fear your anger or your cutting words? Do your wife and children fear you? Would your friends and family say that you are gentle? Would they say that you treat them with tenderness?

Do you like to play the devil's advocate? Do you like a good argument? What would your social media presence indicate? What would the community say or think of you as someone who claims to live for Jesus?

Prayer Points

The God of peace is eager to give you the peace of God (**Philippians 4:7, 9**). So, I encourage you to pray in these ways:

I pray that you would make me more like Christ so I may be gentle like him. I pray that I regularly consider how you have been so patient and gentle with me. I pray you will help me swallow my pride, confess my sins to others, and restore my strained relationships. I pray that you will give me the Grace to be patient and calm when others attack and misunderstand me. Help me respond with gentleness even in the most challenging circumstances.

I pray that I would be slow to begin an argument or to wade into someone else's.

These are suggestions on how to pray. I can't give in to fighting any longer because it grieves my Spirit and causes me to feel uncomfortable.

Imagine being able to watch the apostle Paul in action. How did he treat people, especially those who often failed? In **1 Thessalonians 2:7**, Paul gives us a glimpse of how he treated others: "*Instead, we were like young children among you. Just as a nursing mother cares for her children.*"

Gentleness is a strong hand with a soft touch. I'm sure Paul felt uncomfortable like we all have felt. It is a tender, compassionate approach toward others' weaknesses and limitations. A gentle person still speaks the truth, sometimes even the painful truth, but in doing so, guards his tone so the truth can be well received.

All who are genuinely godly and are genuine disciples of Christ have a gentle spirit in them.

You can't hide it or stop it from showing out to others as a light! It's something God had slowed in you to share and walk in.

The Bible goes out of its way to demonstrate Jesus' gentleness. The Old Testament depicts the Messiah as unusually gentle, telling us that Jesus would not break a "bruised reed" or snuff out a "smoldering wick" (**Isaiah 42:3**). In the Gospels, Jesus affirmed His gentleness: "I am gentle and humble in heart" (**Matthew 11:29**). And the apostles often reminded the early church of Jesus' gentleness: *"By the meekness and gentleness of Christ, I appeal to you - I, Paul, who am "timid" when face to face with you, but 'bold' when away!"* (**2 Corinthians 10:1**).

Unfortunately, too many people equate gentle with weak. Unless you would call the heroic apostle Paul, the fiery Puritan Jonathan Edwards, and the almighty Christ "weak" individuals, it is a misunderstanding to assume weakness has anything to do with gentleness.

The reverse is true.

When my daughter was young, she used to love squeezing my hand as hard as possible, trying to make it hurt. She could squeeze with all her might, but it never hurt. She didn't need to be gentle because she lacked the power to cause me pain. Then, just for fun, I'd give her hand a tight squeeze until she yelped.

The strong hand, not the weak one, must learn to be gentle.

God made me the person I am, with all my quirks, strengths, and weaknesses. But, He also calls us to change and become more like Christ.

He made me loud and outgoing and talkative and welcoming to people. He knows this is me, and even more, He can use it for His Glory. For that to work, though, I had to surrender those parts of myself to His will and direction and let Him refine me. Like the potters' clay, he modes me daily and builds me up!

Gentleness is often used as a positive spin on weakness. But gentleness in the Bible is certainly not a lack of strength but the godly exercise of power. Gentleness does not signal a lack of ability but the added ability to steward one's strength to serve good, life-giving ends rather than destructive, life-taking ends.

"Violence is the destructive use of strength. Gentleness is its life-giving exercise."

> *"Take you wise men, and understanding, and known among your tribes, and I will make them rulers over you."*
>
> *- Deuteronomy 1:13*

"May my teaching drop like the rain,
my speech condenses like the dew;
like gentle rain on grass,
like showers on new growth."

Violent rain does harm, not good. The farmer prays not for weak or no rain but for gentle rain. The means of delivery are essential. We need water (the power for life) delivered gently, not destructively. Gentle doesn't mean feebly but appropriately — giving, not taking, life.

So also, "a gentle tongue is a tree of life" (**Proverbs 15:4**). Gentle doesn't mean weak but fittingly strong, with life-giving restraint — giving something good not like a fire hose but in due measure. Or consider sailing. A gently blowing wind (**Acts 28:13**) answers a sailors' prayer, while a violent wind spells trouble (**Acts 28:18**)

The virtue of gentleness is seen best in God, who "comes with might"! How does he wield his strength toward his people? *"He will tend his flock like a shepherd; he will gather the lambs in his arms; he will carry them in his bosom, and gently lead those that are with young."*

Violence is the destructive use of strength.

Gentleness is its life-giving exercise. Look at the strength and power God has given you. What resources do you have with his Holy Spirit and power? Look at (**Acts 1:8**) *"Once you have received the Holy Ghost, you have received power."*

Those are the Bible's words and promises. To my understanding, being gently passive to others is a gift and blessing. Some of us have different views or beliefs that detour us from the light of truth and reality. If we believe in the Bible, we should follow what it says, right? That is not always easy to follow the fruits of the Spirit or always show kindness or generosity with kindness.

"We want leaders with strength and power, not to use against us, to our harm, but to wield for our good, to help us."

My 13-year-old daughter doesn't want a weak daddy. She wants me to be strong — and to use that strength to help her, not hurt her. And what she needs most is not for me to flex my muscles over her. It's clear enough that daddy is bigger and stronger. She needs to see that I'm gentle. That her daddy is not only strong enough to protect her but that she can trust me to use my strength to serve and bless her, not harm her.

Weak men are often preoccupied with showing and talking about their strengths. Powerful men give their energy and attention not to show off their strength but to demonstrate their gentleness. They can exercise their manifest power for others' good rightly. Insecure men flex and threaten. Men who are secure in their strength, and the strength of their Lord, are not only willing but eager to let their gentleness be known to all. **(Philippians 4:5)**

CHAPTER 9: SELF-CONTROL

"I made a covenant with my eyes not to look lustfully at a young woman."

– Job 31:1

Being Single and Struggling

What does the word tell us about self-control and avoiding sexual behavior?

Living as both single and sexually faithful might feel impossible. For someone single, committing to live within God's boundaries seems foolish in our current culture's celebration of sexual 'freedom.' But Christians find comfort in knowing our loving and holy Lord has a design for every aspect of life. Jesus is always present to help us stay the course of the race of faith, and he constantly holds out forgiveness and mercy when we fail. Jesus and the Bible are wise and practical regarding our street-level fight against sexual sin and temptation. Jesus stands ready to help when we turn to him as we face struggles and temptations.

So let's consider one crucial tool in this battle to help us as single men and women: identifying and fleeing triggers.

In addictions, the concept of a 'trigger' is significant. It refers to people, places, experiences, and things that stir thoughts, feelings, memories, and desires connected to certain behaviors.

A food addict may be triggered to overeat by the sight of pastries or criticism from a parent. A TV addict may binge-watch while significant work is left undone, triggered by feeling lonely or work-related stress.

A trigger prompts a person to move towards a harmful behavior that soothes or numbs troubling and painful life experiences.

In other words, it's a temporary painkiller. But then the pain comes back, stronger than ever. And a cycle is set up. It's never a walk in the park or easy to say no when the flesh craves the desire to trust the past against your better judgment to say no to sin. I struggle daily with not bowing down to my natural nature. Yes, it's so true because all of us are fighting this fight together as we see face to face in the world of opportunity to say no to those choices that will hurt us in the long run. It was so painful to see myself and my family members suffer from my own mistakes that landed me in a different place that caught my decided attention to slow down and accept the fact that I had to change the mindset of living like a loosed man watching and hearing about the cross rather than carrying the cross and living it! It's hard to accept change or rejection from self to bury the old wounds and continue faithfully in the new walk.

As I said, it's a daily challenge to identify the new you in the Spirit that grows like a mustard seed trying to become a whole man of Christ and win souls. More remarkable than he who is in Christ than in the world. This is one of my favorite verses. I always used to remember it until I found myself struggling to read the word and forgetting the thought of that reminder he was still there talking to me and walking with me.

I seem to get stuck in this battle of fighting the good fight of faith, wanting to through in the white towel and give up! Sin is a killer, and lust is worse than draining if you ask me. My eyes are opened to this world of choices and what is needed to remain faithful and grounded to stay away from the dangers of sin!

Paul's statements about why I do what I do and hate the very thing I like to do is bodily honest and open. Sometimes I am not honest with myself or want to be open about myself to others because of the embarrassment or feeling that others might think I am a hypocrite or fake. I have learned to become transparent and accept that I'm not perfect or grounded like Jesus was.

We are only human; I keep telling myself and making excuses to fall into the pattern of sinning again; it's like my repentance becomes numb and lacks strength and power!

Actually, in **Acts 1:8,** God said, "When you receive the Holy Ghost, you receive power!" My power felt weak at times and just unbearable when I needed it.

Romans 7:1-25 is incredible because it's a learning lesson for myself and talking to myself for the thought process to see my weakness and struggles that sin will always be present near me and around me. Is it in me still? Is this why I am talking and writing about it or struggling with it?

Sound familiar?

Like Paul, many Christians, speaking of themselves, find themselves in a similar spiritual battle. We want to do what is right but struggle to overcome our rebellious, sinful nature. We fail, we falter, we do the very things we hate and know are wrong, and when we mess up, we can often grow weary, disheartened, and even overwhelmed.

We ask ourselves:

Why is following in the footsteps of Jesus so hard? How come I can't stop lusting or feeling dirty inside?

Why do we do the things we know are wrong? I know it's not good for me or my confidence to press forward and grow as a mature Christian man to help and lead others.

Why do we continue to sin when we're supposed to be redeemed, new creations in Christ Jesus? The Bible tells us to walk as wise men and not as fools redeeming the time because the days are evil. I hate this feeling of backsliding and wavering the football field as if it's a fishbowl to swim in sin and never find a way out the stadium doors of sin!

Do you ever feel trapped and drained by this desire?

Well, all of us reading between bible pages for directions is wise. Don't give up or let more of this temptation become your downfall!

Paul attempted to address these many questions, describing the battle between sin and righteousness and the all-important, life-changing power of God's Grace.

What Does 'What I Want to Do I Do Not Do, but What I Hate I Do' Mean?

Amazingly, even a Christian as mature as Paul understood that just because we love the Lord and delight in His ways, it does not mean that we are perfect or will always obey Him. Paul went so far as to call himself the "chief of sinners" (**1- Timothy 1:15**) and a "wretched man" (**Romans 7:24**), recognizing that, though God's way is spiritual, he was not (**Romans 7:14**); this sounds like me, and it blows me away when I see more of my sinful nature thinking I had it all together because I was far from the growing point of walking away from this lust of the flesh that easily won't untangle me from sinning as if I had a license to sin!

Yes…. I am saved and believe and confess my Savior Jesus Christ.

Even redeemed Christians make mistakes because we are at constant war with our old, sinful nature, which is fighting to reclaim its place of influence in our lives. Our sinful nature climbs back into the driver's seat when we sin, steering us away from God.

Do you ever feel this way? Are you stuck in a battle waiting to win or feel you will lose it? That's how I feel daily once I have given in to this nasty desire to sin again. We must have self-control over anger, passions, lies, laziness, and, most of all, lustful desires of the heart!

This is why Paul wrote, "*If then I do that which I would not, I consent unto the law that it is good.*" (**Romans 7:16**)

I'm sure some or all of us have this struggle.

And how do we know we have sinned and are being steered away from God? God's word, the Bible, which Paul refers to as the law of God.

The law of God is what exposes sin and shows us where we have fallen short of the glory of God (**Romans 3:23**). Unfortunately, when we examine our lives by this law, we see just how warped, cracked, and imperfect we still are, and next to the law, no one is without sin, not even one! (**Romans 3:9**)

This is why in (**Romans 7:1**) Paul places such prominence on the doctrine of *Grace*. Can you even imagine what Paul's face and his thorns in the flesh caused him to want to give up? We all have those thoughts. There had never been a time I wanted to give up without a fight knowing that I was bought with a price. Jesus tells us by his stripes that we are living again and that his hope is healing our Spirit.

Under *Grace*, Paul argued, believers are free from the law's condemnation. This doesn't mean that the law is useless or obsolete or that Christians have the freedom to keep sinning and doing whatever they want. (**Galatians 5:3**)

After reading and studying the word of God, I have learned that "The law may discover sin, and convince of sin, but it cannot conquer and subdue sin." Forgiveness, redemption, and the power to overcome sin in one's life can *only* come through the power and forgiveness of Jesus Christ, which is freely offered to those who come to Christ through faith. (**Hebrews 9:14**)

As a man who desired holiness, Paul hated his many sins because he longed to be more like Christ. His sin was a reminder that no amount of spiritual knowledge, willpower, or hard work can save a person. I used to think that doing well at work saving money, and so forth, was the way to be saved. This thinking was blind growing up because all I thought was treating others as you like to be treated was to be saved.

I did picture Jesus on a cross, but I thought that was just a simple reminder of being good to others. How foolish and young I was in my thinking. Do we blame this on parents or those around us that have not bought the good news to our attention? Do we point fingers as Adam and Eve did in the garden, blaming each other and the Devil for their faults?

It's the work of the Holy Spirit that can only transform and redeem a stubborn, rebellious heart, and only Christ can conquer sin in one's life. "*Who will set me free from the body of this death?*" Paul asked, "*Thanks be to God through Jesus Christ our Lord!*" (**Romans 7:25**)

Saved once and for all (**Hebrews 10:10**), we are being transformed into the perfect, holy image of Christ *over time*. It can sometimes be very frustrating and lonely in my personal life, but I remember that avid tells us never to feel alone or abandoned because he is right next to us always. The feelings and emotions can make us feel without his love, compassion, peace, kindness, Self -control, and being saved by his mercy.

I know we don't deserve his mercy after we have cut corners on Jesus and disobeyed his righteousness and forbearance. We are like filthy rags before him, and his mercy is a blessing in my life! We should never complain about anything and be thankful for everything.

Released from the law is being married to Christ!

Paul's statement influenced my actions to take a better turn and be alert that I am not out of order with God's will for my path in my faith.

Do you not know, brothers and sisters—for I am speaking to those who know the law—that the law has authority over someone only as long as that person lives?

For example, by law, a married woman is bound to her husband as long as he is alive, but if her husband dies, she is released from the law that binds her to him. Now, this is Paul's statement, and most believers turn and twist this command around into their underground thinking! I say twist because it's their understanding, not what Paul's reading tells and warns us to heed.

When disconnected from the scriptures, we seem to put the different scriptures in place of our understanding. Remember, we are not saved for being friendly, treating others with compassion, moving forward after a divorce, or leaving unrepentant disagreement.

What I am saying is that through my own marriage/ divorce, it was challenging to vision it all falling apart because the day before getting married, we made a beautiful value never to separate or let no man or woman convince us that we are not suitable for each other! What happens years later, and what has taken place to let emotions & feelings detour the commitment to live? We all ask questions and want answers, right? Some of us think we have it all together with the correct answers; what does the Bible say about this?

How does Paul get moved by the Holy Spirit, explained to the church and us?

Let's look clearly into what he said:

So then, if she has sexual relations with another man while her husband is still alive, she is called an adulteress. But if her husband dies, she is released from that law and is not an adulteress if she marries another man.

So, my brothers and sisters, you also died to the law through the body of Christ, that you might belong to another, to him who was raised from the dead, so that we might bear fruit for God.

For when we were in the realm of the flesh, the sinful passions aroused by the law were at work in us so that we bore fruit for death.

But now, by dying to what once bound us, we have been released from the law to serve in the new way of the Spirit, not the old way of the written code.

The law is not saving any of us. Sin is in the way!

What shall we say, then? Is the law sinful? Certainly not! Nevertheless, I would not have known what sin was had it not been for the law. I would not have known what coveting was if the law had not said, "You shall not covet."

But sin, seizing the opportunity afforded by the commandment, produced in me every kind of coveting. For apart from the law, sin was dead.

Once I was alive apart from the law, but when the commandment came, sin sprang to life, and I died.

I found that the very commandment intended to bring life brought death.

For sin, seizing the opportunity afforded by the commandment deceived me and put me to death through the commandment.

So then, the law is holy, and the commandment is righteous and good.

Did that which is good, then, become death to me? By no means! Nevertheless, so that sin might be recognized as sin, it used what is good to bring about my death so that through the commandment, sin might become utterly sinful.

We know the law is spiritual, but I am unspiritual, sold as a slave to sin.

So, Paul states that it's not good to play with sin, stay around it contemplating on it, or give thoughts to its passions.

It brings spiritual death and confusion in my life after committing lascivious acts or sinful gratifications that bring grieving to my walk in Christ.

Yes, it's a daily battle, and I know my weakness is a learning tool to discipline my flesh to obey the Spirit in me.

My favorite verse is "Greater than he who is in me than he who is in the world"!

Sometimes I don't feel like that man or walk like that man. It's like a daily calendar of 31 days throughout December, sinning all month long and attending church on Christmas to give thanks! Where are my heart and steps with Jesus? Can I become a new man in God without this habit of the sin of intimacy and falling by the wayside? What is Paul's aim here for all of us?

Let's see his teaching here. That explains me! Remember that honesty is the spiritual way out of our poisonous lustful passion. Of course, we have different thorns in the flesh and temptations to face.

(We can break free)

I do not understand what I am doing. For what I want to do, I do not do, but what I hate, I do.

And if I do what I do not want to, I agree that the law is good.

It is no longer I who do it as it is, but it is a sin living in me.

For I know that good itself does not dwell in me, that is, in my sinful nature. I desire to do what is good, but I cannot carry it out.

I do not do the good I want to do, but the evil I do not want to do—this I keep on doing.

Now, if I do what I do not want to, it is no longer I who do it, but it is a sin living in me that does it.

So I find this law at work: Although I want to do good, evil is right there with me.

For in my inner being, I delight in God's law; but I see another law at work, waging war against the law of my mind and making me a prisoner of the law of sin at work within me.

What a wretched man I am! Who will rescue me from this body that is subject to death?

Thanks be to God, who delivers me through Jesus Christ our Lord! So then, I, in my mind, am a slave to God's law, but in my sinful nature, a slave to the law of sin.

Now that's Paul's testimony, and he is sharing a sincere relationship with himself and his struggles with us so that we can hold on to what's fighting us inside. Is it because of the flesh? Or is it because of passions and desires? I always ask myself this because I'm dealing with the same issue Paul explains here in **Romans chapter 7**.

I have no idea what Paul's weakness is or what the Bible says it was. But he speaks highly about a fight and struggles to do better and release the desire to not give in to temptation.

Identifying

For a single person battling sexual temptation, it is crucial to identify the triggers that prompt us to move towards pain-reducing behaviors like viewing or reading pornography, crossing physical boundaries with a person, or engaging in sexual fantasy and masturbation.

Let's be clear: married people also must battle sexual sin! Anyone who tells you they have never battled these areas of sinful struggles is not being honest with themselves! However, singles committed to walking in sexual integrity do not have this context for sexual expression, so fleeing sexual temptation will never involve having God-blessed sex such as married persons enjoy.

Now it's a very sentimental topic to some because most Christians think it's okay to have sex with your partner before marriage or being in love.

How do we identify triggers and if we are wrong or right?

Emotions and feelings – What emotions are most troubling to you? Which are difficult to 'sit with' or bring to the Lord in prayer? In addictions counseling, the class is often used to teach that feeling hungry, angry, lonely, or tired are common triggers that addictive behaviors serve to soothe or numb—boredom, sadness, and relational pain. Sexual sin (with people, self, and technology) often attempts to avoid internal pain in our lives, which is usually tied to external, troubling situations.

Circumstances – What situations often precede your fiercest battles with sexual temptation? I find it as working and hanging out in places I should not be. Sometimes, women or friends are not acceptable to God's ways or his Holy Spirit. Bad company corrupts good habits. (**1-Corinthians 13:33**) my favorite verse, and at times I don't always stick by its rules and demands to follow.

It's just like Paul said in **Romans 7:9** about the flesh and its passion for craving the natural things of the flesh, and that's when sin kills and becomes a Harden heart of practice if we are not careful in our walk with this confession. Relationships can be very troubling and have downfalls as well.

Do certain people or relationships trigger troubling feelings for you consistently? In the past, I had a lot of toxic relationships that took a toll on my future experience in dating before being married or divorced.

Not all relationships will be redeemed or 'safe' for us, so identifying individuals we need to avoid can be challenging for Christians to consider.

After all, aren't we supposed to love our neighbor? Yes, and sometimes loving God and loving people wisely (**Philippians 1:9-11**) means being aware of relational dynamics which pull us away from Christ rather than towards him and obedience.

Wisdom will necessitate having firm boundaries with people with whom you have participated in sexual sin; those who constantly tempt you towards lust and selfish fantasy; people who consistently discourage and disrespect you and your boundaries; and those who are manipulative, deceptive, and hurtful with their words. I know how this can play out because I have done it myself, finding fault in falling by my flesh and heart to sin. It's a vast Red flag to walk towards lustful desires because sin kills, and it's not a good feeling.

We must be reminded to look back at times and see the downfalls of our nature and setbacks to not fall again into this trap!

I know that seems like a lot to keep track of, but with focus and intention, it can become second nature. Learning what the triggers are in these three categories will help you not just know what to avoid; you can make those triggers the things that prompt you to run to Jesus, which is the best part of doing this.

Identifying triggers isn't meant to make us live as suspicious, joyless Christians who avoid people or good gifts! The goal is increasingly running towards Christ and away from sexually sinful activities, which we use to soothe difficult experiences. I know it's easy said than done! I already failed in many ways in my past with these temptations and desires.

We can get through these stepping stones if we look at the cross as a way out and see the pain Jesus is suffering on the cross for all our sins and faults!

We need to understand that when we use things repeatedly to get through life, those things we use become our functional gods. They become idols to which we run, they become the things we worship, and that's no different than what Israel did when they ran to and worshipped idols made of wood or clay.

If you remember the Old Testament and all the desires and looking to other things as gods and not the real God was horrified and blindfolded if you ask me.

It's no way to walk away from those places in your life if you are not paying attention to his real voice. Can you imagine being stuck in a place full of strife, confusion, hate, harassment, and any peace around you?

I've been there, and it's not a good feeling because it affects your health and thinking! Your faith becomes a numb feeling, as if you never had faith. I had to fight my way back home as in the first baby steps back to the word of God and let go of this continued setback that kept me sidetracked in my mind. Self-controlled needs to be from the Holy Spirit, not self or anyone else. It sounds so straightforward, perhaps even commonplace.

It's not a flashy concept or a beautiful idea. It doesn't turn heads or grab headlines. It can be as seemingly minor as saying no to another Oreo, French fry, or milkshake; being diabetic is troubling, and not seeing well.

My eyes started fading away thinking it's age, but my health and being blind to what I put into my body—or another half hour on Netflix or Facebook checking out the daily gossiping or bad blogs—or it can feel as significant as living out a resounding yes to sobriety and sexual purity. It is at the height of Christian virtue in a fallen world, and its exercise is one of the most challenging things you can ever learn to do.

Self-control – No punches pulled, no poetic twist, no sweet irony. Self-control is simply that important, impressive, and nearly impossible practice of learning to maintain control of the beast of one's sinful passions. Yes, it's like a monstrous desire to have your own body take direction and bring you into a ditch where you cry to get out, wondering how you got there. What does this really mean? It means remaining master of your domain in good times and when faced with trial or temptation. Self-control may be easier said than done. It's very challenging and hard-pressed if you are not grounded in bible studies or belong to a close church family. I see it as a helpful guide to follow through when your own body yells against the good in you who wants to do right!

Alongside love and godliness, self-control is a significant term for Christian conduct in full flower. It is the climactic "fruit of the Spirit" in the apostle's famous list (**Galatians 5:22**).

One of the first things that must be characteristic of leaders in the church (**Titus 1:8**). Acts summarizes the apostle's reasoning about the Christian gospel and worldview as "righteousness and self-control and the coming judgment likens "a man without self-control" to "a city broken into and left without walls." (**Proverbs 25:28**)

I felt out of control in many ways, and the next morning woke to a broken spirit, thinking I had lost my love for God and sinning stings the heart for sure when you love God and your new walk with him. When it's hindering and tempted not to have self-controlled behavior, it's a warning ahead saying stop, think, react, and change direction! It pulls at your innermost being and waves desires to walk right into a different place than what you stepped closer into. Just a kind of feeling that I have expressed in other struggles that brings me nothing but regret!

"True self-control is not about bringing ourselves under our control, but under the love and mind of Jesus for safety!

The idea of controlling myself presumes at least a couple of things here: 1) the presence of something within us that needs to be bridled, 2) the possibility in us, or through us, for drawing on some power source to restrain it.

As I said, it's easier said than done, but we can complete the taste and the fight; we all are dealing with. When I became a Christian, it was confusing, new, and exciting. For the born-again, our hearts are new, but the poison of indwelling sin still courses through our veins. I ask God at times in struggling weeks or days dealing with sin or my distance from it that He is aware of what it can do to me. God tells me it's nature, and it takes its course for sure.

It's always a fight and Not only are there evil desires to renounce altogether but good desires to keep in check and indulge only in appropriate ways.

Christian self-control is not always the way you want it to be. It involves "control over one's behavior and the impulses and emotions beneath it." I remember reading the Bible letters to Timothy and Titus about these warnings. It includes our minds and emotions — our outward actions and our internal state.

Heart, Thoughts, Actions, Drink, And Sex: Find Your Source And Work Out Your Salvation.

There are many ways to be sidetracked and pushed to many distractions and distancing!

For example:

The children who succeed turn their backs on the cookie, push it away, pretend it's something nonedible like a piece of wood, or invent a song. Instead of staring down the cookie, they transform it into something with less of a throbbing pull on them. If you change how you think about it, its impact on what you feel and do changes. That's a thought I always was told through my father, who was never around, but he used to use this as an example to hear and let my Yes be yes/ and my No Be No! Not snaking and out of control and wanting more as my eyes see what's suitable for my flesh!

This may be an excellent place to start, but the Bible has more to teach than this experience or example, right? Turn your eyes and attention, yes, not to a mere diversion, but to the source of actual change and absolute power outside yourself, where you can lawfully indulge.

The key to self-control is not inward but upward. Entirely riding the horse and not falling off and giving up. A righteous man would fall seven times for his sins, get back up, and start over. This does not mean we willfully sin and have this verse to say it's okay. (**Proverbs 24:26**)

What's Your Gift And Security?

Proper self-control is a gift from above, produced in and through us by the Holy Spirit. You can't buy it or take someone else's gift or security. Until we own that it is received from outside ourselves, rather than whipped up from within, our effort to control ourselves will redound to our praise rather than God's. There are a lot of places that are at war with these gifts and jealousy in the church, and we all have this foolish five virgin's story in the Bible that reminds us that we couldn't give our light away to a dark light that's unsaved, right?

We can shine bright and share the fantastic security of one's calling but can't give it to a tunnel that's still dark when you walk out of it, right? You can shine the place with your appearance, that's it!

We are light to the blind. I thank God for this gift because it's his mercy on my life to have it, and I have held stronger to keep it by my side and in my life to carry me this far to share my experiences and desires to write and pursue my testimony.

But we also need to note that self-control is not a gift we receive passively but actively. We are not the source, but we are intimately involved. We open the gift and live it (walk, talk, act, behave). Receiving the Grace of self-control means taking it all the way in and out into the exercise of the Grace.

You may be able to trick yourself into some semblance of proper self-control. You may be able to drum up the willpower to just say no. But you alone get the glory for that—which will not prove satisfying enough for the Christian. It won't last, and I have lost this way trying to do this on my own until I awaken to know that it's a gift and we want Jesus to get the glory. We want to control ourselves in the power he supplies. We learn to say no, but we don't just say no. We admit the inadequacy and emptiness of doing it on our own.

There is no way to win or stay closer to Jesus without his steps rather than ourselves. We must be followers of his steps, walk his life, and speak his language all the time!

We pray for Jesus's help and secure accountability, and then we thank him for every Spirit-supplied strain and success and step forward in self-control. We will need it all, and without it playing a role in our lifestyle, we can't be moved or guided by his greatness to succeed as faithful witnesses of his Grace.

CONCLUSION

We each desire to walk with God and reap the benefits of our relationship with Him. Our walk with our Heavenly Father results in godly fruit in our lives and hearts, filled with joy and peace. The benefits and results of walking with God far outweigh a life of not walking with Him. Through my own experience I have felt the pain and suffering without God by my side. It's a very disturbing fight without him feeling present in my life.

Psalm 38:4 tells us to taste and see that the Lord is good. I did not know how to do this or start tasting until a dramatic impact had to accrue in my path of growing as a youth. When you taste the goodness of God, you wouldn't want to go back to a life without Him. It is because of the benefits and results we experience when we walk with God – now and forever. Those benefits are feeling his presents and power!

Walking with God means that you are blessed, and you have access to His great promises, which He has given in His Word. A life with God is one of righteous living because of the transformation that comes by His Spirit, who lives in us.

Before I go deeper into the topic, I will address the surface issues and dig further as I go along. Our relationship with God begins when we become born again and continues to eternity. God has given us eternal life, and this life is in His Son, Jesus Christ (**1 John 5:11**). We will be with God now and even after we leave this earth. We know the Bible tells us this all through his word right? It's a matter of belief and faith in this conversation right!

There are many benefits of being in a relationship with God. For example, He forgives your sins, heals you, redeems you from the pit of hell, crowns you with love and compassion, and satisfies your desires with good things (**Psalm 103:1-5**). The result is an abundant life that bears fruit for the Kingdom of God. He forgives your sins and prison past and crimes committed against his will and commands.

No one can deny that our walk with God has many benefits in this lifetime and the next. To benefit, it means that there is an advantage that comes out of something. My own experience has proven this fact and this is why I'm sharing this very important fact of the benefits here. The benefits of God are available to those who have a relationship with Him. We will explore five benefits of walking with God and how they affect our lives. They have sure affected my life to abandon sin and opened my eyes to the 9 fruits of the spirit and how they now affect my life in a higher calling.

1. Eternal Life

One of the best benefits we have of walking with God is that we can be sure we have eternal life. That is the life that goes beyond the one we live on earth to the one we will live in Heaven with God.

A classic Bible verse that reminds me of one of the best benefits of walking with God is **John 3:16**. It tells us that God loved the world so much He sent Jesus to die for us so that we will not perish, but have eternal life. Our relationship with God is never-ending because we become part of His Kingdom when we get born again, and His Kingdom lasts forever. That was hard and difficult to believe or come to light to my blind way of living. What happen that woken me up from a dead life to a life of abundance and fruits to enjoy.

2. Divine Wisdom

Our human wisdom has no comparison with the wisdom of God. I use to think I knew it all and had it all, When we have a relationship with God, He puts His Spirit in us, who then gives us divine wisdom (**Colossians 1:9**). He enables us to live a life that pleases Him, and we bear fruit in the work that He has called us to do. It's a fight for life and a struggle for abandoning a troubled spirit.

Divine wisdom helps us increase our knowledge of God so that we can trust Him more each day. We need the understanding that comes from the Spirit of God because we sometimes face situations where we don't know what to do. We seem to run to others for anything to solve the issue.

When you don't know what to do, or you have confusion in your mind, ask God to fill you with the knowledge of His will.

Only God can move you from confusion to clarify your thoughts in a positive direction!

3. Access to God's Promises

We see in the Bible so many things stated that if we follow him that we can't lose hope right! The promises of God are "in Christ" (**2 Corinthians 1:20**). As a believer in Jesus Christ, you can ask that every promise given to you by God in His Word, be fulfilled in your life.

God wants Us as his children to live the abundant life that Jesus came to give us (**John 10:10**). When we declare God's promises into our lives, they manifest and bless us tremendously, and the glory goes to God. We never get that glory or anything because it all goes to God. I use to pat myself on the shoulder thinking I did it all and it was all me. "*Meet Me Halfway*" is a book I have written. It speaks on taking actions in helping Jesus see your hand reaching for help rather than laying there not trying to reach his calling in your life. He gives the glory and we give our lives to meet him for acceptance.

4. Hearing God

Many people ask how one hears God, and this is because they don't understand how it happens.

We hear God speak through His Holy Spirit, Who dwells in us. If he can speak to me in a jail cell and get my attention, he can do the same for you and others who face a serious negative impact in their lives. Before Jesus left the earth, He told His disciples that they had the ability to recognize the Holy Spirit, because He would be with them and in them (**John 14:17**). It means that every child of God can hear God speak to them anyplace doing a suffering time of crying out for help. He hears the honest tears of your heart.

We long to hear God speak to us every day because we know that He has amazing things to tell us about our lives. He knows more about us then we know ourselves that's for sure.

Hearing the voice of God is comforting, and it reminds you that you have a loving Father who cares about you and will always be with you.

5. An Ordered Life

When you walk with God, your life is organized and orderly because God orders your steps. **Proverbs 20:24** says that the Lord directs our steps, or in other words, when you walk with God, you shall always go in the right direction. Of course, the devil will try and take us down the wrong path, and sometimes we take that path, and God is still there fighting for you and wanting us to come back and turn from being deceived or misleading from other forces that are not of his will, but your own will.

Those who walk with God know where they are going, and they don't lose their way in life. Isn't it great to know that the Lord is by your side, and if you are on the wrong path, He will redirect you? You may not always know where God is leading you, but you can be sure that you will never get lost.

Milton Keynes UK
Ingram Content Group UK Ltd.
UKHW010043220823
427262UK00014B/301/J